"Kristine Ellingson's memoir is one of those books that once begun is read to the end knowing the journey will be fascinating. Filled with rich details of both ancient and modern Mayan life, it is also a love story of a woman in love with life, with family, with creativity and with generosity of spirit and exploration. It's also a story of a woman who took the risks necessary to fall in love with her true self. I'm hoping *Tales from the Yucatan Jungle* is only the beginning of the answer of what happens next."
~ JANE KIRKPATRICK, award-winning author of *Homestead: Modern Pioneers Pursuing the Edge of Possibility* and *A Daughter's Walk*

"From her experiences with Curanderos (healers), to J'meen (shamans) appeasing the Aluxes (spirits) who guard the land, to participating in traditional rituals for the dead and dying, Kris offers a rare, insightful, and fascinating look into the world of the modern Maya in a small Yucatan village. With keen observation skills, incredible experiences and the understanding of a woman who has straddled two worlds for over two decades, Kris is able to see and describe the wonder, beauty and mystery of the Mayan world around her. Her book offers a gateway into a land that we tourists often visit but seldom see."
~ CATHY WILCOX SPARLING, retired Director of General Services, Legal Department, City of Toronto, Canada

"Her love of the place, its color and vibrancy and even its food and its people comes out strong. For me, this book is all a vibrant and descriptive explanation of Kristine's life and life decisions during a time of change.
"What impressed me, and what comes through in the book, is that Kris keeps her sense of humor throughout. One can tell that she takes her life seriously but also accepts what is thrown at her without prejudice and criticism of a different culture. What many might think of as problems or blocks, Kris sees more as a (self) learning situation. She keeps her perspective of life and offers descriptions of both good and bad experiences with a touch of humor. For me, humor is one of the most important survival traits as an outsider. She is accepting of the unknown and the strange and absorbs it all without judgment.
"Life is short. Take chances and be open to everything. One can learn from anything. The serendipitous-ness of life is very evident in this book."
~ SHEILA MATTHEWS, Institute of Nautical Archaeology, Turkey

"I first visited this part of the world over 40 years ago in my red Volkswagen van and have been a regular visitor ever since. In spite of being fortunate to live and work with my wife in different parts of Africa and to study in Europe, I have always retained a strong affection for the Yucatan and its people. We also are both always excited to meet and connect with people who are successfully living 'bi-cultural' lives. Kristine is a masterful story teller who brings this part of the Mayan world alive to our imaginations while at the same time revealing herself as a woman who passionately, and successfully, makes a choice to begin new life at forty-four!

"As I read the book, I not only was fascinated by the stories of her life she shared and her insights into the Mayan life of Santa Elena, but I gained a whole new appreciation for Kristine's skills as a consummate storyteller. And I came to appreciate the courage of her adventure. I know her as a skilled and welcoming innkeeper, a person of passionate interest in the Yucatan and the Mayan people, a woman with a wonderful artistic sense and, by reputation, as a very successful jewelry designer. Now I appreciate her as an individual capable of making life-changing decisions and living out the consequences of her choice, experiencing both the challenges and the joys that brings!"
~ MICHAEL GRAHAM, lifelong student of Mayan culture

"Reading her book I laughed out loud, cried and marveled at the person I was re-meeting. It was wonderful to revisit Kristine, Santiago and Rosa in the pages of this marvelous book."
~ HULENE MONTGOMERY, Michael Graham's lifetime travel companion and Social Development Consultant

"What Kristine has accomplished is truly amazing. My childhood neighbor left her country and family at age 44 and built, through sheer determination, a beautiful compound and garden, learned two languages, educated a village, and in doing so found love and support with a Mayan family. Her intellect, artistic abilities, and work ethic all come together in her accomplishment. In fact, you could say that "accomplishment" has been her life theme. Read her book and go visit her B & B."
~ JANET BAKER, retired teacher, traveler, and a lifelong sports person.

*Donna —
The best of life to you —
Kristine*

Tales from the Yucatan Jungle

Life in a Mayan Village

by

Kristine Ellingson

*Ye'etel Ki'imak o'olal
(happiness)
K=*

SunTopaz LLC
Light Overcomes
Foster, Virginia

Tales from the Yucatan Jungle
Life in a Mayan Village

Published by
SunTopaz LLC
P.O. Box 123, Foster, VA 23056
www.SunTopaz.com

Publisher's Cataloging-in-Publication
(Provided by Quality Books, Inc.)

Ellingson, Kristine.
   Tales from the Yucatan jungle : life in a Mayan village / by Kristine Ellingson.
   p. cm.
   LCCN 2009931127
   ISBN-13: 978-0-9754691-8-7
   ISBN-10: 0-9754691-8-5

   1. Ellingson, Kristine. 2. Visitors, Foreign--Mexico --Yucatán (State)--Biography. 3. Mayas--Social life and customs. 4. Mayas--Religious life.   I. Title.

CT120.E45 2012   920.009'04
                          QBI11-600140

Edited by Clair Balsley, Miriam Balsley, Cathy Hunsberger, and Carol Chapman
Cover designed by Miriam Balsley and C.A. Petrachenko
Cover photographs courtesy of Kristine Ellingson, Miriam Balsley, and Carol Chapman
Internal photographs courtesy of Kristine Ellingson, Sheila Clark, Santiago Dominguez, and Nidia Alvarado

This book is available at quantity discounts for bulk purchases.
For information, call 1-757-810-5347

*To Santiago and My Mayan Family and
to My Two Children, Eric and Clair,
for Letting Me Go*

Contents

Acknowledgements

This book could not have been written without the help and support of my Mayan family and our many village friends.

Prompted by questions from Carol Chapman, all of us started remembering bits and pieces from our lives together, and the stories grew.

The girls went through all their personal photos, allowing me to use many of them. Lucy loaned me one of her lovely daughter, Marta, in her gorgeous *Quince Años* gown.

Neighbors contributed their memories and helped with the spelling of Mayan words.

In return, part of whatever this book generates in sales will find its way back to the village. It may be with new school uniforms or shoes, for those without means to purchase them, a new tool needed for specific work, medicine, or perhaps a computer for the schools. We could think grand and dream of a volleyball and basketball court with bleachers for everyone to watch the games, as we had long ago. People of all ages played and participated, even grandmothers and small children.

Whatever form it takes, the gift will be a thank you to the village for allowing me to experience this life.

A serious thank you also has to go to five very special persons: Susan Goudy and Sheila Clark for encouraging me all along, Nidia Alvarado for her computer expertise, and a special thanks to Miriam Balsley for corralling my verbs.

And most of all, thanks to Carol Chapman. Because of Carol, this book is not moldering in a file in my desk.

Foreword

Through the years, my friend Kristine wrote me a number of amazing, descriptive letters about her remarkable life and experiences living in a Mayan village in the Yucatan jungle in southern Mexico. I have often told others about Kris and some of the colorful stories she shared. I am pleased her accounts are now permanently documented for many more to enjoy.

I first met Kris in 1965 during our freshman year at the University of Oregon when we were in the same sorority pledge class. When I look at photos of Kris from that year, she looks Scandinavian, blond, and very young, although I think we all looked young. During our sophomore year, we had adjacent rooms in our sorority and became good friends. We were both native Oregonians and from rural backgrounds. Kris was bright and quite capable of doing just about anything. She had the best to show for her scrappy childhood growing up near her family's lumber mills in Eastern Oregon.

Kris was serious about her art, had great clothes and ... an extremely messy room. Some of us teased her about her room, and finally, while she was out one day, two of us cleaned it. When she returned from class, she was definitely surprised. We didn't own up to our deed for some time, unsure if she would be angry. She wasn't.

After graduation, we both married and became teachers. Kris was living in Portland, and I was in Eugene. We were both busy working mothers, but we kept in touch through letters and occasional visits.

Kris's jewelry design career began with her creation of simple jewelry pieces produced in her garage and progressed to pieces of fabulous design that received national recognition. She was generous and gave me several pieces of jewelry through the years. I enjoyed following her design progress with each improved, stunning piece.

In addition to her own jewelry design business in Portland, Kris also designed for Zell Brothers in Portland and Sexty's in Boise, Idaho. She owned and ran three Zell Brothers repair shops in the Portland area. She was invited to numerous invitational jewelry shows throughout the United States over a period of several years.

The last time I saw Kris while she was living in Portland, Oregon, she was driving a beautiful car and living in a lovely art-filled hillside home complete with its own aviary to house her collection of rare finches. We went shopping. Kris was looking for an antique Thai silk jacket, and I was looking for shoes. It seemed to me that she had all the trappings of success but seemed intensely driven and unhappy.

It wasn't long after that visit I heard she was in the Yucatan, Mexico. When I began receiving her riveting letters about her new life, I could not reconcile the intelligent, driven, successful businesswoman I knew with the person living in the Mayan jungle writing those story-filled letters.

Kris had been living in Santa Elena, Yucatan, for several years when I first visited. I was working with a women's Habitat for Humanity team in Guatemala and flew to see her in the Yucatan when I finished. I was so excited to see Kris, nervous because it had been so long since our last visit, and intensely curious about her new life. After making it through Mexican customs in Merida's airport, there stood slender, blond, Kris, next to her husband Santiago, a handsome, dark-skinned man with a smile that split his face.

We drove an hour south to Kris and San's home in Santa Elena. Kris' letters had not prepared me for their lovely, spacious home with marble floors, gorgeous arches, and vine-covered porches. My first impressions were of warmth, humidity, exotic birds, flowers, trees, geckos, and fireflies. However, what was more impressive than the surroundings were the changes in Kris. She was more relaxed than I had ever seen her, and she seemed truly content. She was busy with children, designing metalwork for Santiago to construct, running the only bottled water business in the area, helping women from the village start an embroidery co-op, and cooking with her daughters in the kitchen. Here was the smart businesswoman I remembered, and she was happy.

My husband, Brad, and I have visited Kris and Santiago twice more in the past six years. We have come to know San as a kind, engaging, and generous person. Their partnership allows both of their lives to flourish.

This is a story of one woman's second chance at composing her life. In order to do that, she traveled far from her Oregon roots to find home. That her unique and inspirational story is being shared brings me joy.

Lolly Tweed
Educator, counselor, and Kris' friend

Introduction

I realize this is probably an unorthodox way to write a book, but since I have rarely followed the rules, I see no reason to start now.

The following pages are stories and events. They are all true, but they are written from my personal point of view. They are not written from a scholar's standpoint of Mayan culture, as a research project, nor from any professional viewpoint. It is simply life as it happened to me, living in a small Mayan village here on the Yucatan Peninsula.

The people are real and the emotions are real. There is nothing fake about this. I did not set out to write, but stories formed in my head and would not go away until I put them on paper. Some chapters have been a sheer joy and easy to write, some have been exceedingly hard. Putting this all into type at the public e-mail store proved quite taxing at times.

So I hope you find the following stories interesting. They show a small slice of a very different way of life, here in Mayan Yucatan.

Chapter One
An Ibis among the Frijoles

The *papagayo* trees are in bloom again. This happens every year when the winter winds begin to blow. *Papagayos* are kites. Not fancy, colorful, exotic kites. Just kites made out of any old plastic bag, with a little stick frame, the plastic tied onto the frame with thread. Tails are made from thin strips of old cloth, tied end to end, some mixed with strips of plastic so they produce a whirring, rattling noise when airborne. The kites have a fatal attraction for trees, and for weeks the trees will bloom with squares of colored plastic. Power lines will be adorned with string and kite tails. Every kid on the block is out on the street making and flying his kite. This is a man-boy sport, not a woman-girl sport. Girls do not fly kites here. The boys fly them across the main highway, never mind the occasional truck or car antennae that may snatch them away. Any place that is open will do. The area around the church is a favorite since the church sits alone on top of a hill.

The air above our house is full of squares of color. I count seven now. We need a control tower. The *jabin* trees, a relative of the oak, with their clusters of tiny, sweet-smelling, pale pink flowers, have already caught one kite—a black one. Two more kites are draped around our roof water cistern, tails flopping over the side of the house. Another has just nose-dived into the tall, stately ramón tree, one of my favorites because it is always leafy and green. Another black kite is wrapped up in the huge bougainvillea vine that has climbed up through the *jabin* trees that surround my tiny lagoon. When all the leaves have fallen from the *jabin*, the trees will still be wearing their *papagayos*, surrounded by red bougainvillea petals.

I am up on the roof, putting up yet another line of wash. We wash by hand here, using a *batella*, the old Mayan-style washing sink. This is a long, squared-off, oval slab, with a six-inch recessed basin formed just past center, leaving you with enough room to pile dirty clothes on the left side, and the washed clothes on the smaller right side. These used to be made out of wood, but now are formed from a mold, using an aggregate concrete substance. This is raised to hip level, and placed on an angle for easy water removal. The sun is our dryer.

It is a day of such purity as to make your heart stop. The sky is a clean, clear blue. The breeze is cool. Kites are fluttering, birds are chittering away in the nearby trees, and soft ranchero music floats up from the village. Dogs bark, flocks of Aztec parakeets sweep overhead screeching. Carmen, my mother-in-law, is beginning to slap tortillas on the grill in the cooking hut below. It's hard to be sad down here, hard to be depressed. The sunshine and the brightly colored flowers—bougainvillea and hibiscus, flame trees and tulip tree—burn it away. The people laugh it away. They have smiles that can split open the sky.

Ibis is the Spanish word for lima beans. These are fresh ones, pale green in color. However, to the Maya of this area, there is only one kind of bean: black. For instance, *xpelon* are not considered a bean. They are just simply "*xpelon.*" They are a black-eyed Susan bean to me. But no, beans are black. They are not red, kidney, pinto, navy, lima, nor any other kind. They are black. The Spanish word for beans, *frijoles*, can only mean "black beans" to the Maya. The others are *chafa*, fake, something masquerading as a bean.

The Maya are dark brown, short, jet-black haired people. I am Scandinavian—green-eyed, dark blond, tall—a *Norte Americana*. I am about as close to an *ibis* as you can get. My Mayan husband calls me, "The *ibis* among the *frijoles*."

My lovely rooftop garden showing the view of the church from the roof.

I live in a small Mayan village at the base of the Puuc hill range in Yucatan. My house and the huge old Catholic Church are the only buildings built on hills. We face each other, South to North, across the village. I have been here nineteen years now. The church has been here for 350. We have each been hit by lightning several times. Hurricane Isadora blew down one of the enormous old wooden front

3

entry doors of the church. It took 30 village men and boys to hoist it back up again. The slightly higher hill behind my house protected us that time. The storm sort of jumped over the top of us. It hasn't always happened that way.

I share my house with my Mayan husband, his mother, and one of his nieces. In the past, it has sheltered his father, his daughter, his sister, a couple of his nieces, and others. It is a good house.

*   *   *

This area of Yucatan was familiar to me. I used to come a couple times a year, initially with my first husband (my American husband) and our children, and later with a woman friend. Finally I came alone.

Chapter Two
Windows of Opportunities

I loved Yucatan. It caught my heart, just as Portugal had years ago. But Yucatan was closer to home in the United States.

Although most of this narrative is about my life in Yucatan, my story as an adult really starts in Oregon, U.S., where I got married to a perfectly nice man, had two wonderful kids, and had a very successful career. Since my extended stay in Yucatan has so much to do with the house I built—my fourth house as an adult—I think it makes sense to tell the beginning of my story as it is connected to the houses I had in Oregon.

*   *   *

I had three houses in my former life with my first husband in Oregon.

My first house was purchased shortly after I married with money for a down payment coming from my father. He was horrified by the house we were renting, down in what used to be the gypsy town. This was his way of encouraging us to move.

This first house was a small ranch-style house with a family recreational room off the tiny kitchen and an attached garage. We had almost no furniture. Everything we liked was too expensive. Danish modern had yet to come into vogue. The pieces we did like we felt we could almost build ourselves if we had the tools and a sewing machine. My paternal grandmother had given us a gift of money to buy some furnishings, and we decided to use this to buy the tools and a sewing machine, gambling that we could indeed make the furniture we wanted.

Kristine Ellingson wearing "The Red Queen," 18 Karat red gold, platinum, square-cut rubies, and baquette diamonds. Photo by Joe Feltzman

In Oregon, I had lasted two years as a teacher in the public school system and knew I didn't want to continue that route. So I had free time to sew and design. My husband was pursuing a real estate career and had an erratic schedule at best, leaving me alone with our small son and in need of things to do. My husband had soon turned the garage into a woodworking shop and the car sat out in front. The family room became my workspace.

I was also creating jewelry and sharing garage space with my husband. Our small son was brought up amongst fabric, wood shavings, and jewelry wax carvings. He knew what a casting centrifuge was before the age of four. He loved his highchair. Spoons, forks, and other objects were tied to the chair with string as he thought it great fun to throw these objects off onto the concrete floor, delighting in the noise and watching Mom retrieve them. In those days, he went everywhere with me, strapped to my back in a jerry pack, jumping up and down, and almost knocking both of us over.

The Red Queen, invitational show, Lawrence Gallery, Sheridan, Oregon. Photo by Joe Feltzman

Three years later, our daughter was born, and we had one of my sisters living with us more often than not. It was time to find a larger house. Woodworking had become more than a hobby, and quilting had become full time. I was also designing and selling more jewelry. We needed more space.

About this time, my husband's parents decided to build a new house. They moved out of the old farmhouse they had restored over the years. The house was on two and a half acres and only blocks from a grade school. It seemed ideal, but we needed to sell our small house first. This was decided on a Thursday. After doing some painting, we took out an ad in the local paper and pounded a "for sale by owner" sign in the front yard. The ad came out Saturday. I was making cinnamon rolls when my husband came in with people who were "interested." An hour later and it was a done deal. We had just made a $5,000 profit. This was an amazing profit for the time period, the year being 1973. It gave us enough to buy his parent's farmhouse.

This would be our home, and home to more than just our two children, for the next 13 years. My husband had grown up here and everyone knew everyone. Each spring the neighbors would take bets as to when and where my husband would get the tractor stuck in the mud cutting the new grass too early, just as his father had. Then out would come a neighbor's truck and towing chains, and spring would officially start with the towing of the tractor.

In this house, I learned to make blackberry pies and cobblers, as domestic blackberries gone mad grew all along the back border between us and the neighbors. The kids would pick, and I would bake. We also had mature plum trees. My son would run around with a purple mouth, juice dripping down his chin for weeks as the fruit ripened.

The neighborhood was full of kids. We spent almost every weekend with friends who lived nearby and had children close in age to ours. No one had any extra money so it was all potluck and casseroles. While the men talked politics and work and law, we women were supposed to mind the kids and gossip and fix food. But I was always more interested in the men's conversation than the women's.

Black Tahitian Pearl—natural spinel, gold.
Photo by Joe Feltzman

In between making up new recipes for casseroles, one woman and I began to create sewing projects to sell at neighborhood craft weekends and at smaller art places. We went in together, bought fabrics wholesale, and began machine quilting in earnest. We could do it with the kids around, and it earned us money. We made quilts with themes and little pockets and pouches to hold small stuffed animals and dolls, which became quite popular. I eventually ended up with a showing of several intricate machine-stitched bed quilts in a local gallery.

All through this, I was still pursuing my jewelry making, showing in galleries, now working in gold. I had been given a boost by an art league with the unlikely name of LOCAL 14, a group of women dedicated to the arts and crafts. Their encouragement and a yearly art show helped my jewelry business immensely. It seemed like when the jewelry business was slow the quilt-making business was hot, and vice versa.

Ring of Cabochon Emeralds and Trilliant-cut Diamonds: 18 Karat yellow gold, diamonds.
Photo by Joe Feltzman

But jewelry making was not as easy with children. I was now working with professional supply houses and dealers where children were unheard of. My kids hated going to a sitter or daycare center, so we made a pact. They could accompany me if they were absolutely quiet. No squabbling or bickering or asking when we were going home, or off to the care center they would go. So go with me they did. They were allowed a small non-noisy object, books and small stuffed toys being good choices. Small cars were not good, as one obviously had to make the appropriate "vroom, vroom" and crash noises needed for it to be fun.

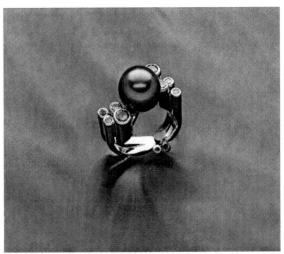

Pipedreams: Black Tahitian pearl, yellow sapphires, diamonds. Photo by Joe Feltzman

So my children were to be found sitting in chairs at Montana Assay, jewelry-finding suppliers, and outside the glass door in the hall of the diamond dealers and the stone cutters. Where I went, they went. Years later, Helen and Bill from Montana Assay would ask about them, remembering all the years the children came along with me. Margaret, from the diamond dealers, would steal out into the hallway to give them cookies, thinking I didn't know.

Our kids were not the only ones occupying the house we lived in. We now had my two younger sisters living with us, one working and one finishing high school. So the kids grew up with young aunties also. As the sisters proceeded to college, my husband decided we ought to have an exchange student to further diversify our lives. Through a church group, twenty young Swedish students were brought over for ten months.

Bracelet, 18 Karat gold, platinum, diamonds.
Photo by Joe Feltzman

That is where we got Olle. Tall and dark haired, from a small village north of the Arctic Circle, he came to live with us at the age of 18. What a crazy year that was. He loved to argue. We would sit on the high kitchen counters and argue politics and whatever else came to mind into the wee hours of the morning.

We also taught him manners. Eighteen is a tough age. You think you know it all and are undaunted by anything. He and his fellow companions were often at the house, tormenting the kids and having a fine old time. I'd come home and find the milk out on the counter, vodka in the refrigerator, and the icebox bare. Very different cultures, but we all survived. By chance, his birthday was the same day as mine. For years afterward, on our shared birthday I would get long rambling phone calls from him, catching me up on everything happening in his life.

The house became a refuge for a great many people over the years and at times a sort of "soup kitchen" during bad storms. When the farmhouse was built, the only other thing out there in the country was a big dairy farm, and we were on the same electrical line. So with a bad storm, we would have power when no one else did. Since we had a gas stove, I could always cook something hot and nourishing. It was here that I perfected my "hurricane soups." People came with their problems and sought the sanctity of the house and land.

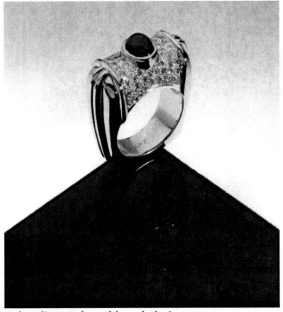

Ruby, diamonds, gold, and platinum.
Photo by Joe Feltzman

During this time, my work in jewelry had been steadily growing in demand. My husband had quit woodworking and went into a computer-generated graphics business. I became the main support of the household while his new business grew. I was doing very little with fabrics now, as jewelry making occupied most of my time.

South Seas gold pearl.
Photo by Joe Feltzman

Soon I received a major offer to join forces with a very well-known northwestern jewelry store in Idaho and Washington State. My work would take me traveling several days a month. The children were getting older and in need of better schools. We made the decision to move once again, this time to a lovely newer house up on the hill overlooking the river with mountain peaks in the distance.

In this last house, I brought my career to its peak. One of my sisters was once again a frequent visitor and guest, added to the various children. My life reached a crescendo of activity, overwhelming me at times.

At the same time, our marriage was slowly unraveling as my husband and I traveled further in different directions. I suggested counseling, but he was not interested in going that route.

All our lives had been particularly hectic. We had two other children living with us, one a Chinese exchange student with minimal English who was attending the same high school as my daughter. The other was a young man who was a friend of my son's whose mother moved to Virginia and forgot to take him. Before he came to live with us, he had been couch-hopping among friends for weeks.

Added to that were all these kids' many friends. The front door was never closed nor was the refrigerator, and everyone needed to talk at one time or another. My ex-husband once told me that "strays" were supposed to be dogs and cats, not children. But I didn't ask for these children. The gods simply placed them on my door, and I couldn't say "No."

And now they were all leaving, to university, to jobs, to the military service. The boys moved out and the girls graduated, one continuing on to university. The Chinese exchange student had been with us for three years now, as well as my son's friend who followed me into the jewelry business and continued successfully on his own.

It was time to face facts. And try to breathe.

Although I had just been offered a fabulous job in the jewelry world on the East Coast, I had told no one. Money was no enticement, nor was I intimidated to think about moving. I wasn't even sure that I wanted to continue in my career. The term "serious burn out" occurred to me more than once.

I suspected that my marriage was completely over and that my daughter would soon be in the Persian Gulf War under George Bush Senior. While the East Coast would bring me closer to my son, it was at a time in his life when he really didn't need "mom" around either.

I realized I was free for the first time in my life to consider and even do this. There was nothing to stop me.

But I needed a place to think and decide, away from all the influences at home—a place with no fax, no phones, no television—a place where I could be alone and decide what to do with the rest of my life.

*   *   *

At a seminar for small businesses held years ago in Washington D.C., an instructor said, "There will always be windows of opportunity in life. These can last a second, an hour, or perhaps a few days, no longer. To take advantage of these, you must be prepared ... prepared and with enough courage to fly through that window and take advantage of the opportunity presented."

Chapter Three
A Slight Detour on the Way to Portugal

I decided to take a "sabbatical." Take a month or two off from my work. Be on my own. See who I was. See if there was anything inside of me. Or was it all just painted on and plastic? My husband agreed to this. Together we had been to many places in the world, both on and off the beaten track.

I knew where I was going. No beach for me. I set off for the hinterlands.
Photo courtesy Santiago Dominguez

I knew where I was going for my month alone. The only place I knew well and would feel safe alone. No phones, no TV, no fax. I flew to Merida, Yucatan, rented a Volkswagen bug, and set off into the hinterlands, to a hotel I knew well. No beach for me. It was January 1991, and I was 44. A month, I thought ... then maybe on to Portugal.

It took me a while to "unwind" from the fast track. My life for the past 22 years had been in the design and manufacture of high quality jewelry ... a hectic, demanding life.

*   *   *

Once I get to Yucatan, I stay at the Mayan hotel where I have stayed before. I know everyone on the staff. They are concerned because I am alone. After about ten days, I begin to wake up again and look around. I decide to learn Spanish. My husband and children speak it, but I have never needed it before. The men on the staff of the hotel have always taught me a little Mayan—that is their language—but no Spanish. I buy a beginners' Spanish book and use a box of flash cards my daughter gave me. I start practicing. I am terrible ... maybe even hopeless.

One night I wander down to the reception desk. It is late. There are almost no other people in the hotel. I need an aspirin. Do I have a headache, or am I just lonely?

A "new guy" is on duty. His is the first new face I have seen in years on the staff, other than the sons of fathers who already work here. I know he is from Merida, the capital of Yucatan, but was born and now lives in the neighboring village of Santa Elena where half the staff comes from. I know his name is Santiago and that it means St. James in English. He has a perfect Mayan profile, just like the ones on the nearby ruins.

He is studying English from an old dictionary. We can't talk because we have no common language, but we look up enough words to understand each other. We both want to learn the other's language. I give him a group of the flash cards. Every night we meet to see how much progress the other has made. Everyone is helping me learn, but I still only know words—words I cannot yet connect.

After five weeks, I go home to Oregon for my daughter's 18th birthday. A brilliant child, she is in her last year at a private high school. She has decided to join the U.S. Navy, starting at base level. Nothing my husband and I say will change her mind. We are appalled, but we have already agreed she must do things her own way. We had always assumed that Clair would go on to university right after high school, as we both had done. But a hotshot recruiter came to the school during her senior year and before we knew it, Clair had joined the Navy. University would come later.

My daughter had come to my rescue one summer when I was forced to join the computerized world. Because I knew nothing about computers, she ran the office for me until I could find help. She was funny, gracious, charming, and fourteen. Now she is a young woman and must decide for herself.

My son was already happily ensconced in the Maine Maritime Academy back East.

Through quirks of fate, my husband and I have raised, or had responsibility for, seven children—only two of which are our own. Now, with all of them gone, and after five weeks of being on my own, I realize that the kids have been a buffer for a long time, a way to avoid reality, to not recognize the gap that has grown between me and my husband. We have been leading parallel lives for a good many years, sharing a house but little else. I even thought it possible that his affections might lie elsewhere.

We take a short vacation to Hawaii, again with various kids, and I am forced to admit that it is all over. I must decide what to do with the rest of my life.

During the three months in the U.S. that follow, I begin to study Spanish seriously. I buy four books: *501 Spanish Verbs*, *Essential Grammar*, *Madrigal's Magic Key to Spanish*, and a huge *Harper Collins Dictionary*, the best in the world. My goal is to learn five new verbs each day. I make a list of essential verbs, ones I am sure I will need to survive. I learn only three tenses: present, past, and future. I bypass the rest for now, certain that I will lose hope otherwise. My children laugh at me. They say I will never be able to do it, learn Spanish this way.

"Give it up Ma, you're hopeless," they say.

But I am *going* to do this. I have decided to go back to Mexico, to Yucatan, for a year, then on to Portugal. But to live in Yucatan, even for a year, I must have some Spanish. I will not be living in any *Gringo Gulch* area, but in or near some small village. This much I have decided.

My sisters think I have gone truly mad.

My pronunciation of Spanish is terrible, but I have some concept of the language now.

I go down to Yucatan in May for three weeks, looking for a place to live or rent. Nothing is available in the small villages I am considering. Santiago, the "new guy" who works the reception desk at night, and Concho, another one of the young men on the staff of the hotel, take me trekking through the jungle to see several old *ranchos* on their days off. These are more like abandoned ruins.

We are not in old hacienda country in this region, like further to the north. We are in low scrub jungle here, cut many years before for farm land and later abandoned for lack of water. This is low canopy tree growth, thick with thorn trees and difficult to get into. The scrub brush quickly takes over any habitation. I begin to realize that to do this, to live here, I must truly make up my mind. Jump off the bridge. Sell everything. Cut all ties. Start over. Do I have the courage? Am I doing the right thing?

I return to the U.S. at the end of May for my daughter's graduation. She takes a zillion top awards. But she is going into the Navy for four years and leaving soon. She will leave home before I will.

I realize that I miss the Yucatan sun. I miss the flowers. I miss the houses that they paint with such gay abandon— fuchsia and lime green, purple with a pink roof line. I am looking at grey—grey sky and grey buildings. Even the flowers aren't as bright in Oregon as in Yucatan.

I miss the music most of all and listening to the flow of their Mayan language. The man named Santiago has given me some music cassettes that I listen to constantly. I haven't a clue what they say, I just like the flow of the music. (Years later, my Mayan family will tease me when I learn that one of my favorite songs by Emanuel is not "*da me chansa Maria*" but "*caprichosa Maria!*") I miss the people. I left my heart behind, and I need to go get it.

But for me to leave, I need to sell my car and my business and also make arrangements for our house. This happens in one month. I sell my business of twenty years, my lovely pearl-grey sports Mercedes that I worked so hard to buy, make plans to sell the house whenever my husband wants, give my clothes away, and pack my life in the three 24" by 18" by 14" boxes the airline permits me to take.

I take small objects I have found or bought all over the world—tiny gifts and treasures that I cannot live without. My red cowboy boots (snakeskin), my sewing machine, photos of my kids, books. I am not coming back, but no one knows that yet. I can't tell my clients. They would want "just one more piece" of jewelry. They would keep me here.

When I decide to leave the U.S., sell everything and go, when everyone says I am crazy, I wait for a sign from "the gods," something to stop me, to tell me I am wrong, to hit me with lightning or something like that. I have always relied on these "signs" to help direct me. But the gods aren't giving me any. Nothing stops me. My business sells, my car sells. I had saved money all my life so I have enough put away. My husband doesn't stop me, my children are happy in their own lives. It is only my sisters who think I am making a big mistake. Therefore, it seems that I am being given a chance. The door is open, and I just have to have the guts to walk through it. And I do.

My children are off on their own roads. Now I must find mine.

My husband drives me to the airport. He says he will come down to see me, but I know he won't. He recently told me he hates Mexico, the Mexico I love. I am numb. I suppose one hopes against hope that something will magically change, that the man you have lived with for so long will once again be the man you fell in love with, but it is not to be. He is letting me go.

I arrive in Merida and am both excited and shocked by what I have done. I will need a car while staying at the hotel, but for now a rental will do. The next day, I set off into the jungle, heading back toward the interior of the peninsula, toward the hotel where I have stayed before and where I will stay again for a while. I plan to get settled in.

Once at the hotel, I take up a sort of permanent residence. Santiago, the "new guy," is helping me a lot. He has learned more English, and I have a little more Spanish. But it's still mostly guess work. We laugh a lot. I am learning some words in both languages, Spanish and Mayan. I quickly learn to swear, like most kids.

Santiago walking to his parents' sleeping hut as I saw it for the first time.

One day, a mini crisis develops at the hotel, and I am sent to the village where Santiago lives to find him. They need him to come in early to help set up for a large incoming group. I am told to wait until he is ready and bring him back to the hotel. In this way, I finally see where he lives. I meet his mother Carmen, his father Indalesio (often called Don Indal), and his retarded, epileptic sister Maria, all of whom he is supporting. They live the traditional way with two palm-thatched huts—one for sleeping, the other for cooking.

I naively ask where the bathroom is as I watch him shave in a car door rear-view mirror hung on the wall. The mirror is so old and cracked I wonder what good it does. There is one bare light bulb dangling from the thatched roof.

Santiago's parents, Carmen and Indalesio.

The only pieces of furniture are an old wooden wardrobe with faded glass doors that close with a tiny key sticking out of the lock, an ancient stereo console that apparently hasn't worked in centuries, and hammocks. Hammocks are used for everything. There are no beds, chairs, or tables that I can see. There is no refrigerator, TV, or radio.

Santiago is embarrassed because they are so poor. I learn he has returned home after 15 years, spent mostly in Merida. He left the village when he was thirteen, looking for work to help support the family. I learn in due time that he has a daughter and small son in Merida, and a bad marriage. He is 28.

Santiago when we first met, in 1991, on top of the church, helping repair the bell.

We become friends. We are both ending our marriages. We both have children we love. I take him to Merida several times to resolve various family problems. He takes me to village events, and I meet more of his family and friends. He has two more brothers, two half-brothers, and a sister. One of them has 10 children. They also live in the village. He is related to half the village! The local doctor is his cousin. One of the trio of singers at the hotel is another cousin. I am invited to weddings and birthday parties.

I slowly become aware that I am very attracted to this man called Santiago. He has no idea how old I am. My age is not apparent like it is on some of the women here.

First village wedding—cousin Elmer.

After weeks I still cannot find a place to live. Nothing. I would have to rebuild everything I have seen. Most places have either no kitchen or no bathroom. Some have neither. I wonder where they cook, where or what they use for a bathroom.

Chapter Four
I Buy Land in the Jungle

One day Santiago's father suggests that I build a house on the back part of his property. I begin to think that perhaps I should be thinking about housing in a different way.

*   *   *

I do not make the decision lightly to accept Santiago's father's offer to buy his land. Don Indal has actually willed the land to Santiago.

The view of the huge Catholic Church from our hill.

None of the other brothers want it because it is *en el monte*–in the hills, out on the very edge of the village. The property is one hectare, about two and a half acres, and even has legal documents, which I soon understand is unusual here.

The back land is all wild scrub jungle. I hack my way back there and realize there is a small hill. I can see the huge Catholic Church from there! And it has motmots, lovely exotic tropical birds native to the peninsula.

These large birds have Cleopatra-black outlined eyes and a flashing turquoise brow-stripe that almost glows in the dark. Two oval plumes of turquoise feathers look to the rest of the world like the plumes are hanging from two pieces of wire. The plumes form the end of the bird's long slender tail. Melodious song it has not, rather sounding like a hoarse dog barking, or maybe a frog croaking, sometimes both. They sit in the trees without moving, occasionally swinging the long tail like a clock pendulum. Hence comes the motmot's Mayan name of *Toh*, meaning clock.

I first saw this bird years ago, sitting dead still in a huge ceiba tree near the ruins of Chichén Itzá, was promptly mesmerized by it, and here it is! The ceiba is considered the sacred tree of the Maya, called *Ya'ax Ché* in their language. In full maturity, it will stand well above the rest of the jungle and can be very large in girth. The tree grows straight up with the foliage opening up way overhead. For the Mayans this tree represents the communication between the real world and the underworld of spirits, a symbol of wisdom and endurance. Its branches open to the four cardinal points and unite these points with the rain and the wind. The branches support the heavens, the roots are entwined in the underworld.

The jungle also has some gnarled twisted thick vines climbing up through the trees that bloom in purple clumps, like delicate lilacs, during the cooler winter months. Small black and white warblers dance up and down the bark of other trees, searching for insects. There is a wonderful dank, dusty, peppery smell to this kind of jungle that I love.

I am euphoric.

Then reality sets in. Why would his father offer this? I know money is tight for them. Is it for the money? What would happen if this didn't work out? Could it be divided? Am I thinking *palapa* hut, cottage, or house? I had originally thought of a small bungalow, just for me.

I spend days at the hotel thinking and drawing. I am drawing a *house*. The design is flowing out of my hands onto the paper. Measurements are there. I don't think in metric, so I "step it off" using three feet to the meter. Close enough. Floor tile patterns are developing, arches form on the terrace, this house is drawing itself. My God, it would be huge! For whom?

Santiago and Concho are assuring me they know the people who can build it. They all have friends, cousins, brothers, uncles, who work in building construction in Cancun or Merida. They will come back to the village and do it.

What am I doing? I need to talk to a lawyer, someone who knows English, land deeds, and foreigners. Much to my amazement, I find the perfect person. But I still need a reason for even considering such a plan.

So here I am, once again waiting for a sign, something to tell me *why* I should want a house, here on this land, with all its possible complications ... and why a house this *big*. I need a sign.

Santiago asks if I can take him to Merida again. I know him well enough by now to see that he is upset about something, so I say, "Of course."

He needs to stay overnight, so I arrange to stay in the city in a hotel where I will be comfortable. I can take him back the next day. He could have taken the bus, but I enjoy the trips, and he knows the city. I am hopelessly lost driving in Merida by myself on the many one-way streets.

I know he misses his small daughter very much. He has shown me her picture. I take him to a park near his old house where he asks me to wait. An hour later he is back, visibly upset. I suggest we drive to the port town of Progreso, 20 minutes to the north of Merida, and have lunch. He then tells me a great deal of the story of his marriage and life in Merida. It is not pleasant.

Santiago's first marriage was to a girl that he thought would be the woman of his dreams. But she turned out to be a Dragon Woman. His daughter Yulisley was born more than a year after the marriage, and Santiago adored her, this child of his. Because his wife was often away from the house, he would feed, bathe, and play with his little daughter.

Santiago was working then in a *Calera*, a place where they pulverize limestone rock to make cal, used in cement construction, which in time ruined his back. Later he worked for a few years for a pharmacy, and finally for a *Cristaleria*, a store that sells glassware, dishes, and kitchenware for hotels and restaurants. When his wife up and left, sometimes for weeks at a time, he had to rely on friends or his sister-in-law to help out with Yulisley. But Santiago wanted this marriage to work, and each time he took his wife back.

She began to drink heavily and fights were frequent. One day Santiago arrived home early to see a man he knew leaving the house in compromising circumstances. It was too much, and Santiago left for good, taking only the clothes on his back. His son was born five years after Yulisley, after Santiago had left, and even though he suspected that the child was not his, he gave him his name anyway.

Santiago headed for Cozumel and what he hoped would be a new life. He had only been on the island a short while when the devastating hurricane Gilbert hit full force, wiping jobs out in its path. It was 1988. He went home to his village to take care of his aging parents and to try to once again pull his life together. Here he finally got a job at a hotel near Uxmal and began work anew. He saw his daughter and son infrequently but Yulisley wrote him letters that he still has today. He always sent money for the children's care even though his wife was living with yet another man, a pattern that kept repeating itself.

Yulisley is six. She misses her father terribly and always wants to be with him. Many times she is alone with her year-and-a-half old brother, waiting for her mother to come home. I suggest he bring her to lunch at the hotel where I am staying, somewhere they can sit and talk. She is a darling little girl, but so sad! She has never eaten at a restaurant before. We are outside on the terrace so it is quite calm and peaceful. This is not a fancy tourist hotel. She is very shy. What must she think of this pale, blond, tall stranger sitting in front of her?

Later we take her back to the park near her house, and again I wait for Santiago to return. He cries most of the way back to the village. I ask him why doesn't he bring her back to the village for awhile? It is summer, and she is out of school. He doesn't think he can because she speaks no Mayan. His mother speaks no Spanish and has full care of the epileptic Maria and the household. He has to work with only one day off per week.

"Well, couldn't one of your ten nieces and nephews help out?" I ask.

Several of them speak both languages, Mayan and Spanish. The nearest in age is Mimi, age seven, a year older than Yulisley. But Mimi is reputed to be a bit of a problem—stubborn, silent, not outgoing.

"But surely for a week it could work?"

Santiago is still on night shift at the hotel, so he would have some time with her each day. I am spending more time in the village, and my Spanish has improved, so perhaps I could help?

Yuli and Mimi.

We agree to try. His wife gives him permission to take his daughter for a short while. So, Yulisley comes to stay with her grandmother. Mimi visits everyday and leaves in the afternoon. The two girls seem to take to each other instantly.

Mimi seems somewhat lost in her large family. She is the middle child and there is a newborn baby too. Two of her older sisters are epileptic, one also crippled by polio, both needing a lot of attention. Mimi comes more often and stays longer every day. Yulisley stays for a month. Her mother doesn't seem to miss her.

I ask Santiago why doesn't he finish his divorce process and ask for custody of the child, knowing how difficult that would be. No money.

We both know by now that there is something serious growing between us, but nothing is said on either side. We have become closer through our trips to Merida and studying the two languages at the hotel at night, where he is still working. We are alone many times, as there is almost no one else staying there. I also realize that because of his lack of education and material position, he is very hesitant to make any suggestions or moves to someone he considers a "Queen."

I cannot imagine what he would want with an older woman when it is obvious that he has many women friends. Meanwhile he thinks of me as a beautiful blond American who couldn't possibly be interested in an "Indian." The difference in our ages bothers only me, it seems, not him or his family. They have all accepted me, all except his half-brother Maximiliano who speaks only Mayan. The rest are very nice and friendly. Brother Antonio is great! Antonio is the father of most of the nieces and nephews. He speaks Spanish as well as Mayan and can even understand most of my beginner's Spanish. I am in the village now most days, driving back and forth from the hotel where I am still staying.

The new baby, epileptic sister Maria, center, and Yuli, right of her.

When it is time for Yulisley to go back to Merida, she threatens to "run into the hills and never come out" if she has to leave. She wants to stay with "us," myself being included in that "us."

"Why can't we just all live together and be a family, with Mimi too?" she asks.

*   *   *

The other shoe dropped ... right on my head. The sign I had been waiting for. Was this the reason for the huge house? Was I going to marry this man, a man seventeen years younger than me, with a family I could barely communicate with? I felt I was where I was meant to be, and I knew I was happy ... as I felt he was. His mother had said that this was the first time her son had been happy in many years. Would I have to make the first move? I could only hope the gods would look down with favor this time.

But, I had no idea what I was in for. My sisters thought I had gone completely off the deep end. My children were having trouble understanding me but were coping well enough. My divorce was almost finalized. I was about to start a whole new life.

Chapter Five
I Build a House

The house I am building is huge. The people here think it is a hotel and keep asking what the name of it is.

*   *   *

Mayan houses are about three by four meters, at most five meters long. My house will be eighteen by twenty-two meters. I am not used to metric. I soon find all the conversion factors I need in the back of my huge Spanish/English dictionary that I brought with me from the U.S.

I want tall ceilings, big windows—screened with wooden louvers and no glass. The people think I am crazy to want windows so big with no glass—the spirits can get in.

Santiago's cousin Juan is in architect school, so he draws the formal plan for the house from my drawings. I soon learn that no one will really use the plan he makes as they can't read.

By now, Santiago and I are living together in a small motel in a larger nearby village. As it turned out, one night at the hotel, I simply didn't want to stay alone. It seems he didn't either.

To oversee the construction of the house, we are driving my newly purchased Nissan truck back and forth each day. Santiago has quit work at the hotel to oversee construction on the house. No one in the family seems upset by our decision to live together. No real declaration or proposal has been made between us, it has just kind of happened. Maybe we are both too afraid of the relationship not lasting, so we take it a step at a time, going very slowly, each learning about the other. That he is extremely intelligent and kind becomes more obvious every day.

Over the summer, Yulisley and Mimi plus Cousin Alexandra sometimes stay with us. No one seems to think that this is an odd arrangement either.

The girls all fall out of their beds. They have only slept in hammocks.

Hammocks are wound around roof beams during the daytime in the sleeping hut. In the background, Carmen's grown daughter Pilar and Yulisley second from right.

Santiago is the acting "coordinator" between me and the construction work crew. Most of the crew speak only Mayan. They do not work with women. Here, women make no decisions of any consequence outside the household, but I don't know that yet.

At night my brain sizzles and pops. Sometimes I can't seem to think in any language at all. I learn about *vigas* and *bovedillas, alambre cocido,* and *clavos*—kilos of *clavos*. These are beams and concrete blocks, annealed wire, and nails. I have designed the rooms around the tile sizes and the length of the concrete support beams. Exact ceiling width and height is decided by the size of the concrete blocks.

The door and window makers are in Merida, as are most of the other suppliers—tile, plumbing, bath fixtures, lights, stoves, beds, refrigerators. There are countless trips buying and hauling things home in the truck. It is amazing what you can get in the back of a small Nissan truck, a *camioneta*, as they call it here.

View from the new house location—looking north toward the village—clearing the land of trees and vegetation to start.

There is no earth-moving or concrete-pouring machinery. We remove large rocks with huge metal stakes, pickaxes, and dynamite. Somebody yells, "*Bomba!*" and we all run inside the thatch houses below to avoid possible falling rocks. Several come through the roof in the process.

We are clearing and forming a road up to the site where there was once only a slight trail through the scrub jungle. The workers put down over one hundred meters of hand-laid rock roadbed, hand-carried to the site. Each rock is laid in precise rows, one after another, three meters wide, with sascab over the top—eventually packed hard, like white concrete.

The cistern, under construction, to save water in the future.

Sascab is the white limestone "dirt" we have, along with solid rock, all over the one hectare plot of land. We dig a hole and remove sascab to form the large cistern that will hold rainwater for the house. We then place the sascab, which was excavated from the hole for the cistern, over the rocks on the newly forming road.

We must build the road to the site as soon as possible. It must be strong and solid enough to support the huge trucks which will bring the thousands of concrete blocks and mountains of *polvo y grava*, sand and gravel that, along with bags and bags of cement, will form the house.

We blow up the rocks. They become the foundation of the house. There is no way to level the land here, other than by hand. The front of the house is on solid rock, so it stays. The back part is actually built on two large squares filled in with thousands of more rocks that we pay someone to bring in by truck.

Building the road to get there—all of it.

I have chosen the best quality of concrete blocks and the good sand for the construction. The men are impressed. It is more luck than anything. I know nothing about this kind of building. In Oregon, houses are made of wood.

We are going to have bathtubs, wonder of all wonders, and hot water heaters. I will use the gas oven to bake, not to store my dishes in, like everyone else does here.

For the people in the village, the oven space keeps their dishes stored and clean. It is good protection against dust, insects, and mice, for those lucky enough to have such an appliance.

They ask, "Can you cook?"

"Yes," I answer.

I can sew too. My sewing machine traveled here with me in the overhead luggage compartment on the airplane.

Our motel room with the sewing machine on one table, my layout designs for the house on the other.

I have complicated my life again. At the same time as I'm designing and building my new house, back at the motel at night, I am sewing dresses for my new girls. I have moved in two metal tables from the bar/restaurant: one for sewing, one for design and layout. Graph paper and colored pencils are everywhere. I make patterns for the dress parts out of pellon (a thin interfacing material) to try it on the girls. I have never sewn without a real pattern before.

*   *   *

Over the years, I have made hundreds of dresses—Cinderella dresses, graduation dresses, bridesmaid's dresses, pleated skirt school uniforms, costumes for Carnival, and First Communion dresses. All are more complicated and exact than has been seen here before. I teach two of the daughters to sew very well and how to use math to figure out the number of pleats to a skirt, how to employ math in various kinds of sewing. These two girls go on to make most of their own clothes.

Carnival costumes all made by hand.

*   *   *

When I realize the construction workers can't read, I draw and color in the floor tile patterns for each room in the new house. I have made the designs too elaborate, not just squares. They can't understand what I want, so I draw each design, hand color it, and color code it to the tile colors and sizes. I have complicated my life yet again.

Rose comes to stay with Grandmother Carmen also. She is the oldest of Brother Antonio's ten children. Mimi is her younger sister. Rose is almost the same age as my daughter in the U.S., eighteen. She comes to help with the girls and to help cook, also to help care for Grandmother

Carmen, Santiago's mother, who has suddenly landed in an American whirlwind of activity. By the end of October when we move into the new house, Rose moves in with us and becomes my third new daughter.

Rose in the carnival costume she made herself.

My son Eric comes to visit and everyone instantly falls in love with him. He is twenty. My daughter Clair is now in the Persian Gulf.

*   *   *

My son returns several times, and it is he who will help me form a water collection system using PVC tubing to catch the rain water off the roof and store it in the big cistern for use in the house. He will also teach the village boys to jump the topes, *speed bumps, at high speed on their bicycles, much to the boys' delight. Carmen cries each time he leaves. So do I.*

Eric and the girls and their Merida cousins.

*   *   *

For the construction of the house, road, and cistern, we actually have fifty-six people working for the first couple of months. The main core of about eighteen to twenty men, the "magicians" who make this work possible, are all from the village. They usually work large projects in Merida and Cancun but have returned to the village to do this project and to have more time with their families.

I come to know certain people well. One I call "Michelangelo." He is the fine-finish concrete worker with the unpronounceable name of Leodegario. His brother Julio is also here. Both are cousins to Santiago. Watching them is like watching artists at work. Amalio is the plumber and electrician.

Armondo and his brother Abelardo have the most beautiful gold-toothed smiles you will ever see. I learn from Armondo that when he asks if I want something done

45

a certain way, he is actually giving me hints. If I say no, and he says nothing, I learn I am about to make a mistake. For instance, Armondo asks how I want the tile wall molding done. I can't see why we need it (it would be fancy wood baseboard molding in the U.S.). He says nothing. I start looking at hotels where we stay in Merida, as well as restaurants and business places. They all have a tile wall molding at the base of the concrete wall. I ask Armondo about it again, and he tells me that the way you clean tile floors here is to throw on buckets of water and Fab, powdered detergent, sweep it around with a broom and then squeegee it out the door. The tile wall molding keeps the concrete wall from getting wet and falling apart.

About two weeks after starting the house, with the base foundation in.

"Well, yes, then I think we should do that," I say.

Now we will need more tile. Back to Merida.

We end up putting marble in the main bath for the floor and sink counters. It is a lovely color that comes from a nearby quarry on the top of the hill going to Ticul. The marble is cheaper than the tile at that time. Another cousin quarries and cuts it.

A cousin works for the door and window company in Merida too, so the owner comes out to take all the measurements when we are ready. In time, we have lovely solid cedar doors and window frames and louvers that fit perfectly when they come to deliver and install them, all in one day. They cost almost as much as the whole house!

The inside of the house showing what will become the living room. The men are in the present breakfast area.

I think I want wood cabinets for the kitchen, and wood closets, until I learn that cockroaches *love* to hide in wood areas like that. We quickly decide to do it all in tile and leave everything open. We have never had cockroaches. I am learning.

The house is not without mistakes, but most of them are rectified in time. For example, I come in one day to find a huge high opening for the main door, almost to the twelve foot ceiling.

"Why is it so high and wide?" I ask.

"Because we have heard that North Americans are very tall," they answer.

"Yes, but we are not expecting Paul Bunyan here. Eight feet will do nicely."

We break out a few concrete blocks and fill in the rest of the top and side space. I learn they have a plan to make all the door sizes different, nine of them, for "variety." I standardize them all, and the cost goes down.

Front and side of the main house where the arched terraces are now.

The next time I come to the house site, they are preparing the counter areas in the kitchen. The Maya here are short people. I tower over many of them, but to use these counters I would either have to be sitting down or bent way over. We raise all the counters and the little girls will all have to learn to stand on chairs to help cook and cut vegetables.

Sadly, the main bathroom tub faucet will forevermore have a strange elbow in it where the water pipe comes out of the wall, instead of behind the tub where it should be. I got there too late that day. It had to be made to work somehow. No one had ever seen or installed a bathtub, let alone this strange curved faucet.

*   *   *

I have now been here some time. I will soon have a house, three new daughters, a man I am living with, a future mother- and father-in-law, and fourteen new family members just in the village, not counting cousins, uncles, and aunts. A whole new life. What in the world have I done?

**In our first year, not married, October 21, 1991.
(Ah yes, I smoked then.)**

One of my sisters had said that I was running away. I was not running away, but I was running to. Running, as fast as I could towards this new life I was being offered. I was running before someone or something could slam the door shut in my face—this door that had been opened so suddenly in front of me into another world.

Chapter Six
About Getting Lost

I am now teaching Santiago to drive. When I bought the truck, a used one, not one of the sales agency persons, all men, would get in with me to test drive it. They went in the back and obviously drew straws to see who had to go with the crazy Gringa, sure that we would all be killed. Women don't drive. They were also horrified to find that Santiago could not drive. What else will I learn here in this new land?

*   *   *

It is payday for the construction workers tomorrow so we must go to the bank in Merida. Since we have so much to do and so many purchases to make for the house, we decide to stay in Merida for the night. We always stay at the same place. They know us well. They have seen us, after shopping, lug in boxes and sacks of towels, sheets, dishes, pots and pans. We back up the truck, loaded with a stove and refrigerator, to the door so the night watchman can see it and guard it. They have become a kind of family over the past two months.

Santiago does not yet drive well in the city so I am driving. We get to town late and the bank takes forever, but finally we have everything and are heading back to the hotel. We are in the center of town—the old part—a maze of buses, cars, trucks, people, and one-way streets. People with small sidewalk fruit stands are packing up to go home, leaving orange and mango peels heaped in the corners of buildings. The day is sizzling hot and exhaust fumes are thick in the air. Long lines form at the bus stops for those lucky enough to be heading out. It is almost 5:00 p.m. and shops are opening again after the afternoon siesta. People are swarming like ants. It is a nightmare to drive, and it will get worse.

I have never been able to make sense of Merida, to find my way around. I grew up with mountains and rivers, tall "buildings and towers" you could see for miles. You could orient yourself easily, even if you didn't know exactly where you were. You weren't truly lost, just a little off course.

Merida is not like that. It is as flat as a pancake, as is much of the Yucatan Peninsula. There are no high buildings or towers. Nothing exists that is visible for miles, let alone blocks, and so Santiago always tells me where and when to turn.

Just after we leave the bank and enter the worst part of the old section of town, Santiago suddenly remembers he did not pick up his father's sandals. They are being resoled again. His father doesn't want new ones, they will hurt his feet.

We are stalled in traffic, mashed together like bumper cars, so Santiago says, as he is jumping out of the truck, "Just go around the block, to the right," and is gone.

"Wait!" I yell, but he has disappeared, gone into a labyrinth of small shops and stalls.

Traffic begins to move, but I can't cross the lanes in time to turn.

"I'll go another two blocks and then turn right," I think.

I have to go two blocks before I can turn to the right because of the one-way streets. But at that intersection, there is a policeman waving me to go straight. I can't turn.

I am a little nervous. It is late afternoon and darkness comes quickly here. Boom! And it's dark. I also have all the money sitting in my handbag beside me. The side window is open in the truck, the door unlocked from when Santiago jumped out. I know it is not a good part of town because he always walks behind me here, to prevent an assault or robbery. I stand out like a sore thumb among these people, and tourists do not come to this area. Santiago used to work in this part of the city and knows it well, but I do not. He never leaves me alone here. The truck door and window are too far for me to lock and close. Traffic is too heavy, I can't stop.

Suddenly, I am by the post office and I shouldn't be. I try to think of where I have come from, how many blocks, how many turns. I make more turns and there is the same policeman again. So I am close, but I still can't turn right and have to go straight. I try a different way and there is the policeman again!

I see a hole in the traffic flow and pull over. The policeman signals me, "No, no," but I don't care. I am lost. He is a policeman and is supposed to help me. Those are the rules. I march up to him with my lousy Spanish and try to explain that I am lost. I can't find my husband. The policeman doesn't understand me, he doesn't have time, and his job is to direct traffic, not to help some bimbo North American he can't understand anyway.

I have tears in my eyes by now. I am getting a little frantic. A man comes out of a small store and asks in mangled English if he can help. I try to explain what has happened and where I need to go, but I don't know the number of the street nor the shop name, nor any of the shops' names where Santiago jumped out. I remember only parked buses and stairs going into a building.

"*El Mercado del Artesanías?*" the shop owner asks.

But I don't know. He draws me a map on the hood of the truck and indicates where I must go. He wishes me luck. I wipe my tears away, thank him, and begin again.

Soon I am back at the same corner with the policeman! How can I keep finding this same corner and nothing else?

It is dark now, pitch black here in this poorly lit part of town where I shouldn't be but can't manage to escape. Both the store man and policeman are visibly concerned now. They are talking together about what to do with me. I am crying silently again, exhausted from the day, the heat, the noise. The shop man apologizes that he can't take me anywhere, he cannot leave the shop. The policeman calls headquarters but they won't let him leave his post until 8:00 p.m. That is an hour away. I have been going in circles for almost two hours.

I decide I should just try to find the hotel, get out of here—the old section of town. But the shopkeeper and the policeman don't know the hotel where we are staying.

"It is by the airport," I say, "on *Itzaes, Avenida Itzaes.*"

They draw me another map, wish me luck again. I drive and drive. I am now out of the heart of the city, but nothing is familiar. It is residential, one long line of buildings with different doors to indicate separate residences.

Finally I see a woman and her small son waiting for a bus. I stop and ask her if she can help me, give me more directions. She considers, and then says, yes, if I will take her to her house, she will help me. She lives close to the airport.

They climb in the truck. The small boy is afraid of me and sits on his mother's lap, as far away as he can get from this strange white person. We drive for many blocks in what feels like the wrong direction.

Suddenly she says, "This is my house."

She indicates where I am to go next, but I don't understand it all. She speaks too fast and my Spanish is too poor to grasp it all. I thank her.

At least I am on the outskirts of the city. I know somewhere I will hit the *periferico*, the highway ring that goes around the city. I come to the big old stadium Kukulkan and realize I am way to the southeastern part of the city when I should be in the southwest. I ask at a drugstore and, in two blocks, I am on the inner *periferico*.

"Go to the Coca Cola plant and turn left," they had said at the drugstore.

I am there. I can find my way now, I think.

I finally reach the hotel. It is now almost 10:00 p.m. Santiago has not returned. The people at the hotel are concerned. I go to the bar and tell them to send me a double gin and tonic. The man from reception desk is bringing in the day's purchases from the truck and putting them in our room. When he leaves, he asks if he can do anything more to help. I tell him if my husband comes, to tell him to go to hell, go away, I never want to see him again, I hate him. The reception man doesn't understand my English, but he knows I am upset.

He leaves as I shake my head and reply in Spanish, "No, there is nothing else. Thank you."

After awhile, I order another drink. The bar is actually closed, but they make one anyway. The barman says my husband has come and is running through the long corridor to our room. I order two drinks.

Santiago comes through the door, the color of a sheet. He waited for hours. Then he asked a policeman if there had been any accident, anyone lost. When he finally realized he must return to the hotel, hoping I had found it, hoping I was alive and not lying on some street corner somewhere, he remembered he had no money. I had it all in my handbag from the bank. He didn't even have enough for all the buses it would take, let alone a taxi to the hotel. He had been running and walking most of the way.

I can't even talk I am so exhausted, angry, shaken, and happy to see him again—all the emotions mixed up inside, fighting for which will win. I have been in this country for two months now and reality has just hit me in the face. I am not in the U.S. anymore. I need more language, and other survival skills ... ones I don't have.

I don't remember going to bed. We wake up late the next day. Without a word, Santiago takes the keys and drives. His father's shoes lie on the seat between us. I will never drive alone in Merida again.

*   *   *

I have driven crazy, twisty, narrow mountain roads, spun twice around on one, the girls loaded in the back, an enormous cliff on one side, the earth falling away hundreds of feet on the other, and I did not panic. I learned to drive my Volkswagen bug against suicidal, big trucks and buses on the narrow curve-filled coastal gulf road, learning the signals for when I could pass, slipping in and out of trucks with inches to spare.

But I have never driven in Merida alone again.

Only one other time Santiago said, "Just go around the block, it will only be a second."

"NO!" I said, "If you get out of this car, I will drive to the airport and go straight to Portugal!"

And I meant it.

Chapter Seven
Human Ingenuity

In building the house, I still have one major problem. In my mind, I can't figure out what will hold up the ceiling. How will the concrete blocks stay up there? We have ordered these *vigas* and *bovedillas,* but I don't know what they are, what they look like, or how they work. I know the English words now, beams and concrete blocks, but I don't understand why they aren't just going to drop to the ground.

Uploading the beams (vigas).

When the beams arrive, I suddenly understand the concept. The *vigas* are stepped beams and the blocks sit on the step or lip. The bimbo is learning.

I am told that we must go out into the jungle and cut about a hundred straight long poles. Why? The poles will form scaffolding to stand on to put up the walls. The poles will also hold the beams in place in the ceiling so they won't sag when the concrete roof is poured. If the beams sag, ceiling cracks will form later.

Santiago and his brothers carrying beams (vigas) in the Yucatan heat.

For weeks during this phase, the inside of the house looks like a striped pole forest. A hole is left in the middle of the roof area where men lift bucket after bucket of concrete to pour this mammoth roof monster that I have inadvertently created.

I am appalled when I realize how they intend to pour the roof. There are no big cement mixer trucks here. I am fascinated and amazed when they *do* pour the concrete with the help of a small electric cement mixer we finally find in Merida.

We somehow manage to get the cement mixer into the back of the truck using three guys and a "come-along," rigged up in a big tree to hoist it up and into the truck.

After driving this behemoth mixer back to the site, I then find that no one knows how to use it. We spend the next several hours looking for someone who does.

I don't realize until then that you can't pour a roof in sections. It all has to be done at once or cracks will form where the sections meet.

Columns up and plywood to form the arch area of poured concrete.

All these things I am learning every day, every minute, in two languages. I am also taking care of two small girls and helping with the cooking for the core crew of about eight, who are mostly relatives who eat with us everyday.

The main meal is served at about 1:30 p.m. At 3:00 p.m., work begins again until dark falls. The main meal easily involves eighteen to twenty people, eating in shifts everyday for about three months.

We come from the next village every day, so I help with the shopping, preparing, serving, and washing up. The guys even build a concrete block area where I can wash dishes by the old *pila*, the water storage cistern, instead of washing them on the ground as I have been doing. Later I even cook some of the meals, completely on my own, much to the family's surprise. The *Gringa* cooks too!

As we acquire needed appliances and dishes, these are stored in the living/sleeping compound and in the new thatch structure that eventually becomes Santiago's wrought iron workshop. This structure was originally intended for me and him to live in, Santiago having never inquired if this would be acceptable to me. It wasn't. It became our main storage area, quickly filling with building materials, such as cement bags, which are protected from the rains.

The dishware and appliances go into the sleeping hut, crowded in around the edges, leaving room for hammocks to be strung out at night.

At night, hammocks are strung up around furniture in the sleeping hut.

The new stove enables me to help cook. I make the family muffins and brownies, goodies they have never had, finding out that the dogs love these as much as the family does, stealing them from right under my nose.

I give the family a refrigerator. They use it to make and sell ice, in small plastic bags, to all the neighbors. I also buy them a table with chairs, and a television, things they could only dream about having before. My clothes and linens are stored in boxes up above the wood pole rafters in each of these two huts.

At least my boxes are not sharing space with the *ratonera* snake. This bull snake is a resident of the cooking hut roof thatch, tolerated to keep the mice and rat population down, eyes gleaming as you cook.

Yuli and her Dad, the summer of 1991—San's birthday—Carmen's sleeping hut with a new 'fridge and fan.

The night pour of the roof is the most amazing feat of engineering and human endurance I have ever seen. We start at dawn, work all through the day and night, and finally finish the main part after dark the following day. Bucket after bucket passed from hand to hand, along three levels of the scaffolding, and up through the hole to the roof. There, the cement is dumped and spread with rakes and boards as fast and carefully as possible.

A wire netting has to go down first, over the *bovedillas* and beams, for the concrete to adhere to. So not only do the men have to get these long beams into place on the roof by hand, but they also have to place the hundreds of *bovedillas* correctly before they can pour the actual roof.

Imagine balancing on bouncing scaffolding made of poles and a few boards, the scaffolding tied together with vines and bits of wire, putting up and cementing into place thousands of blocks as the walls rise higher and higher. Vertigo anyone? The men are our very own acrobats, balancing blocks at 15 feet in the air.

Forming of arches—night work—note roof beams in place, some with "bovedillas." Note all the poles and more barely visible inside the room.

I sit day after day and watch in amazement. I am humbled. We Americans have technology, machinery, and all the tools of the "modern world." Yet look what these men can do by hand, with nothing but manpower and ingenuity, in blazing sun or torrential rain, laughing and joking all the way through it. It is such a sight to see, and I record as much as possible with my camera. The house becomes theirs as well as mine, and they pour their hearts and talents into it to make it superb.

I don't understand until well into the project that no one can actually calculate out anything this large. Tiny one room houses, yes, but not this. They have all worked under engineers and architects before. We have neither. Santiago and I become both. I draw and redraw designs, cover page after page with calculations in metric which I have never used except for high school math. I swear fluently in three languages as I wad and tear and toss pages of useless figures that don't work because of some detail I don't know. I think my brain is going to blow up.

Night pour of roof—mesh wire ready to go down, jerry-rigged lights.

The completion of the roof, when at last we get there, takes three days. During the initial first pour, while the men work around the clock, chanting and singing to keep their energy up, we slaughter and prepare on the grounds a huge pig to make *tortas*. These are a kind of French bread sandwich, served along with several dozen cases of beer and Coke. People eat in shifts all night long.

*   *   *

I have photos of all this, from the pig to the men as they wrestle with this huge roll of wire netting and lay it down on the roof. I took photos because I knew I would never see it again, and later, never believe that I, we, they did it. By hand! These people are incredible.

For years, they bring visiting relatives to see "our" house, the house we all built.

We finished the house (or mostly so) in late October 1991, four months after beginning, with a work force of 50-some people.

We started this house-building project on July first. The men worked weekdays from 6:00 a.m. to about 6:00 p.m., sometimes longer, with an hour and a half for lunch. On Saturdays, they only worked until 2:30 p.m., with Sunday off unless we had a complication.

We moved in the second week of October, with 98% of the details complete. It was an incredible accomplishment when you consider the size of the project and lack of equipment and tools. The men used no levels, no plumb-bob lines—just nails dangling from a fishing line and chalked fishing line strung between stakes for determining levels. When I finally bought a level and a square, for my own curiosity, I found that all the walls were perfect, the floors level, and the rooms square.

Chapter Eight
Cooking and Sleeping the Mayan Way

I learned a lot building my house and got many strange looks when I designed the kitchen and sleeping area under the same roof.

*   *   *   **

I learn quickly that cooking is done in a separate thatched hut, made with wooden poles standing end up, close set but not stuccoed over, to allow the heat to escape.

The compound below the new house—the water/power source for construction. Cooking hut left, sleeping hut right. Cement pila (round), center, for water storage.

People ask how these thatched cooking and sleeping huts survive in a hurricane. Actually, they do fine! It is rare that a well-built one will be severely damaged.

In addition, no one will leave their home unless the military literally forces them to. They also refuse to go to a shelter, no matter what, preferring to believe in their own skills. Rebuilding is an effort. You must buy or find the palm for the thatch roof, cut it, dry it, and then weave it into the roof poles to form the roof. These round pole-and-thatch structures are amazingly stable.

The separate sleeping huts are made of stucco over the wood poles, the stucco being formed from mud and *zacate*, a plant looking like corn, which forms a kind of straw when dried.

Rose's family compound, her aunt and three sisters on the right standing in front of their sleeping hut, and me, standing in front of their cooking hut.

Traditional cooking is like camp cooking, the old fashioned way. You have to find just the right size rocks, upon which the "grill" sits, this being typically the top of an old oil barrel. Dry wood for the cooking fire is brought in every few days or as needed. The wood is cut in the nearby jungle. It is this wood, always from a type of oak tree, which gives Yucatecan meals part of their particular flavor.

Many meals consist of boiled food, all cooked in one large pot which hangs over the fire from a chain hooked to the roof beams of the cooking hut. All pots are charred black on the outside, from use, but scoured perfectly clean inside after each day's meal. Typically, a family has one frying pan, one large cooking pot, and one medium blue enamel pot that is used for noodles or smaller meals.

Our cooking hut with one of the neighbor girls.

All families seem to have one or two cutting knives, one fork, and one large spoon plus a ladle. Tortillas are used in place of silverware, with the occasional chicken foot serving as a fork for certain meals.

Drinks are generally passed around in a *jicara*, a dried gourd cut in half to form a bowl.

When cooking, one sits on a *banqueta*, a wooden concave stool/bench placed right by the fire. Because I am taller than most of the Maya, this means that my knees are up around my chin.

A typical Yucatecan Mayan family party held in the sleeping hut—no silverware in sight.

There is always one small round low table with three legs—generally the only table owned—that is first used for cutting up any meat or poultry and/or vegetables. It is then scrubbed clean and used to make the tortillas. These are formed by hand from the *masa*, ground corn dough made only from corn and enough water to make it stick together. The tortillas are slapped out on small sheets of plastic and then cooked on the grill. After the tortillas are ready, this table is used to serve the men first. The women always eat last.

Cooking is rarely done indoors in a concrete house, which in many ways is sensible because of the heat of the Yucatan climate. This way, you do not have to worry about cooking with grease and cleaning it up. Scraps are thrown out to the animals, so there really is no garbage produced. Few people have refrigerators, and if they do, the refrigerators are used for Coke and Pepsi, not food. The food cooked for the day is just enough for consumption. Leftovers do not exist here. The exception is beans, which are sometimes reheated at night to keep them from souring.

Rose and Grandmother Carmen talking and cooking tortillas in the cooking hut.
Photo courtesy Sheila Clark.

This is not a can-opening society either. You rarely see anyone with canned goods, except perhaps for large sardines in a tomato sauce. This is a favorite of the men, especially construction workers (both housing and road construction).

No one would ever, ever buy prepackaged meat from a supermarket. I was told that you only buy meat when you know who raised it and how, what it was fed, and who had actually put it in the package—things that would have never occurred to me.

I also take the word "patio" out of my language forever after learning that it is the word the Maya use for the "outdoor toilet area." This is a specific part of the family compound, no matter what the size of the land, set apart to serve as the toilet. Everyone knows where it is and who might be using it at any given time. It could be just open land away from the huts, a certain cleared space in the jungle.

When the patio is inside the village, in a family compound that would be visible from any direction, a small square low fence-type structure is erected. It is about four feet tall, made from thin sticks of the *huano* palm fronds placed closely together, to give some privacy. When going in that direction, you take a few carefully folded pieces of toilet paper. Being a special guest, I was given a "chamber pot" to use inside the stuccoed sleeping hut.

Bathing is done in the living/sleeping hut by putting up a blanket over one of the two roof beams to produce a modicum of privacy. You have one bucket of water if you are lucky. Cold water. During the colder winter weather, this water is first heated on the cooking fire, especially for older women and small children, and used sparingly. Bathing and hair washing is done every day by everyone at around three or four in the afternoon. After cooking, washing clothes, and working in the fields, the family is then "presentable," ready for company or visiting with the neighbors.

Everyone uses a hammock within the sleeping hut, hammocks being used for sitting and chatting as well as for sleeping. You will never see hammocks slung outside. This

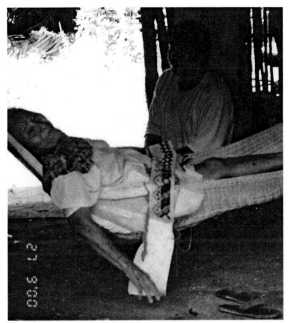

Grandma Carmen with her embroidery, Santiago in shadow behind.

would be much too public. If people are chatting outside, they sit on rocks or the small *banquetas*.

Chapter Nine
Puppet of the Gods

When I decided to come and live in this particular part of Mexico, my allergist was horrified. I have severe allergies to foods, certain drugs, and tons of pollen. At the time I came, I had suffered through several attacks bad enough to require a hospital—or instant injections. I had been on a seven-year-long program of weekly preventative injections to try to build up a tolerance to the worst of these allergens and had to avoid the rest. So my allergist, of course, thought I was signing my own death warrant by moving to Yucatan.

"Move to Guadalajara, then," he said. "They have good hospitals there."

But I didn't want to live in Guadalajara.

I thought, "If you are barely keeping me alive here, in the U.S., what difference does it really make?"

I came anyway.

I have always had faith in the gods, even when I felt as though I were no more than a puppet waiting for them to pull the strings, a pawn in their giant chess games. I would some-times get impatient waiting for them to decide.

"Come on, roll the dice. Let's go," I would say to myself.

When I got no real sign that I was making a major mistake by moving to Yucatan—no bricks dropped on my head, no thunderbolt—I knew the time to decide had come.

"Do you have enough courage to do this or not?" I asked myself. "Can you leave everything behind, all the material things you've worked so hard for?"

I cried as I packed the three boxes the airlines would permit me to take, but I knew I was going. The gods were giving me a chance at a new life, and I had to take it.

I have since learned that there are two things much more important than money and possessions—love and companionship. And they have no price at all. They are free. You just have to find them and allow them into your life.

*   *   *

It is not all fun and games. The first years are not easy. I get everything that comes down the pike from the typical diarrhea to dengue to blood poisoning. I am rushed to the hospital twice for allergy attacks, barely making it each time, Santiago driving like mad to Merida, an hour away. A wet cloth over my face keeps out the pollen from a blooming flower covering the countryside as far as you can see. But I won't give up.

After one severe attack and an eye infection, my eye specialist asks if it isn't all the pollens causing my eye problems too.

"Probably," I reply.

"Why don't you consult an allergist?" he asks.

"I can't find one here," I say.

"Oh a new one just arrived six weeks ago, and I know him," the doctor says.

"Do you think I could get an appointment? Where is he?" I ask.

"Here, in this building, two floors down. Just a moment," and he makes a phone call.

Within minutes, I am sitting in the office of a man who not only saves my life twice, but, by his personal interest in pursuing the pollens I am reacting to down here, sets up a program to "desensitize" me and helps hundreds of other people in the area. Since many of the pollen plants, flowers, seeding grasses, and trees are only known by Mayan names, this doctor has nowhere to start. But start he does, researching Mayan names and finding books until he has the answers.

It takes several years, but finally I do not quake at the sight of field after field of beautiful butter yellow tahonal flowers, source of honey, and formerly lethal to me. I can enjoy the birds who sit in my *katsin, waxim,* and *jabin* trees, even when they are in full bloom, instead of seriously contemplating cutting them down. The trees surround my house and cover most of the peninsula. This doctor, more than any other, allows me to continue to live here in this area that I love.

*　　*　　*

The doctor had arrived only six weeks before I had desperately needed him. The gods must have been watching out for me once again.

Chapter Ten
I Buy a Daughter

Yulisley, age 12, in formal *terno*.

The swallows are back, doing their bombing routines over the roof under the arches, precise as MIG jets, zipping over and around me. When the doors are open, they often come screaming through the house, chittering away. I leave all three doors open so they can sweep through the house end to end. They are mad at me now, I suspect. For years I promised them a water fountain. I never got the fountain, but I did make a small lagoon where they and others could get water. But the lagoon is cracked now and has almost no water, damaged somehow by hurricane Isadora. I must redo the concrete on the bottom to seal it up again. Then they and the flycatchers will be happy again.

The swallows were here about the same time I bought Yulisley, Santiago's daughter. Although she had come to live with us, it was not yet a permanent arrangement. Santiago had to get custody of her, not usual here, or anywhere, for a man to do. His soon to be ex-wife came at the end of the first summer to take Yuli, as we would call her, back to Merida. Santiago and his ex-wife stood out in the small lane outside the palapa *houses below our new house and shrieked and yelled at each other, Yuli crying hysterically. I couldn't stand it. I knew we would lose her. I went up the back way to the house that was almost finished and stood at the top of the road and cried, as I am crying now remembering.*

*   *   *

I am not alone. Carmen, Santiago's mother, has come up the back way too and is standing beside me as we watch the drama from a distance. Soon Santiago's brother Max appears and we all sit down. Max is talking softly in his hesitant Spanish, which I have learned he can speak, not just Mayan. We are standing now, the three of us, and I realize the support I have here and am surprised. We can still hear them below, screaming at each other, and then silence.

Suddenly, I see Yulisley turn. She flies up the road and flings herself into my arms, almost knocking me flat, sobbing, "Let me stay with you and *Papí*," over and over.

A car door slams. Santiago turns slowly and begins to walk toward us. We start running down to him, Yuli and me. He is crying. We all are crying, but we are together.

Yulisley, at a school event, showing a close up of the intricate embroidery on her formal *terno*, made by Rose and her mother Berta.

A decision has been made. Terms given. His wife wants 10,000 pesos to sign the papers for her child, Santiago's daughter. That is a lot of money. More than they can imagine. More than they had ever had all at once.

I know I will pay it.

It is not easy, but in the end we get custody of Yuli until her 18th birthday, the legal age here.

However, things do not work out as well for Santiago's son. He is about three years old when he comes to live with us. Santiago's ex-wife shows up one day in a battered old blue Volkswagen. She dumps him off at Carmen's thatch house in the compound below, steals money from Carmen, and leaves. Other than Yulisley and a father he has rarely seen, the boy doesn't know a soul here.

Typical fiesta meal (again no silverware) with Santiago's son on the left, behind Santiago.

He is as happy as a clam. Yulisley is delighted to have her baby brother with us. I have to say, I am less so. By now we have the water purification plant running full on, the two little girls are in school, and sister Maria has constant epileptic attacks that someone always has to help with. I have my ongoing struggle to learn enough Spanish to cope with an ever more complex set of circumstances, and I really don't need a baby. But you adjust, and there are many people to help.

Slowly but surely he captures all our hearts. He learns Mayan and English, along with Spanish. I read him fairytales in English. As he gets older, he helps Santiago's brother Max wash bottles in the water plant, helps Grandma Carmen feed the pigs, chickens, and cows, rides in the truck with his Dad, and adores playing with his sister and many cousins.

"Blanca Nieve" (Snow White), our first calf.

Santiago's son learns to eat Swedish meatballs and barbequed ribs along with beans and pork and tortillas. We celebrate his fourth birthday with a huge piñata, surrounded by family and cousins. He is about as happy as a little kid can be.

During this time that he lives with us, the school children ask us to do a special Christmas party, and we agree they can use our house. Every year before Christmas vacation, the school children go together singing carols, from house to house. These are Mexican "carols" and probably like none you have ever heard. They carry palm fronds decorated with balloons (they're cheap and readily available) and lanterns made out of old tin cans with shapes cut out and candles inside. One can is used for money which they ask for at every house where they sing. It always reminds me of Christmas and Halloween combined.

Special Christmas party we arranged when the girls were small, Santiago's son at the end of the table with Yuli to the left, and Mimi behind Santiago's son, in the last row.

The money they collect is for the Christmas party, so they very proudly present Rose and me with all the small pesos they have collected. It would hardly pay for a small cake, let alone one for this group, so I have one made in Ticul and pay for everything else. The kids never know.

Then the blue Volkswagen shows up. Santiago's son gets dragged off, kicking and screaming, away from us all. As suddenly as he came, he is gone. Yulisley is hysterical. Max and Carmen cry the whole day. Santiago and I just look at each other. We have no legal rights to the boy at all.

We spend years trying to find him again. He gets left with this friend and that one, never for long. Yulisley is very sad after the few times that she does see him, but we can do nothing.

When Santiago's son is 11, we receive a phone call. Santiago's ex-wife is going to send him to reform school, he has gotten so far out of control.

Santiago brings him home, a sullen, out of shape, belligerent, *angry* kid. So much anger. He refuses to do anything. He won't help with chores, he won't work. His self-esteem is zero. He now wets the bed. He is mean and nasty to everyone, and all five of us wish him gone. Yulisley is his only ally.

This time, it is bad news for everyone. He steals, he lies. He is an entire year behind in school. I have three months to get him up to the level he needs to be in order to enter school here. He and I do three to four hours of school everyday—math, geography, history, and science—the only subjects I feel I can teach him.

Pulling teeth from a live Saber-Tooth Tiger would have been easier. While Santiago puts him to work physically, and teaches and works with him in one way, I teach him another. He is very, very bright, but first we have to get his attention. I invent games and find that he loves Roman numerals. Yes, really, and slowly he begins to respond.

It is a long, long year for everyone. At first he respects no one, then eventually, finally, Santiago and me. It is a really hard fought battle, sometimes physically.

At the end of the year, he is pretty much human again. It is his graduation from primary school. We all go. He has done fairly well in school and has made a few friends. It seems like he might make a go of it after all.

And then Dragon Woman comes back. Spiked high heels, short, short skirt, five ear studs in each ear. She takes him away.

*   *   *

We have seen him twice since. The last time he came by himself for Carmen's funeral. That was two years ago. He gave me a hug. Nothing for Santiago. Santiago's ex-wife had told him that Santiago was not his real father.

We have heard that he is still in Merida. I would wish to God that he had been left with us, but he wasn't. He sometimes contacts his sister.

Chapter Eleven
We Get Married and are Offered a Baby

Whoever said, "Oh, just cross the border and get married"
was truly crazy.

It took us almost a year to jump through all the hoops, get
all the right papers, convince immigration that yes, despite all
odds—differences in age, education, religion, and culture—we
really did want to get married.

*   *   *

Shortly after I "buy" Yulisley, Santiago's divorce papers
are signed giving his ex-wife the house in Merida—a house
he had worked so hard for years to buy. It is the only thing
he owns. He never hesitates a bit. We are on our way to
becoming a family, made of bits and pieces from this
family and that one. Now we need to think seriously about
getting married.

First, I must get an original birth certificate. Okay, get
sister on the line. Now produce *my* divorce papers, which,
oh heavens, are in English! Naturally, I am from the U.S.

"Get them translated."

Where?

A shrug.

Who knows?

We go to the American Consulate and are given a list of
names, most of whom we can't find or who can't do that
kind of legal document. By now it has been weeks of
countless useless trips from the village to Merida. We

finally find a lawyer who can speak, read, and write both languages and can legally translate the document!

Back to immigration.

"Oh, but your name isn't Clark anymore. You are now divorced. You must legally change your name back to your maiden name."

Back to the consulate.

"Do you have any legal document proving you were ever 'Ellingson,' other than your birth certificate?"

No. After almost 22 years of marriage, I do not. Not a bank statement, not a passport, not a driver's license, nor a credit card, not *anything* to prove that I was ever "Ellingson."

"Then we can't help you."

Great. Now what?

My original passport, issued eons ago, was in Ellingson, but that was left behind in the U.S., if it even still exists. More phone calls. It does exist! My ex-husband has found it and is willing to send it. With that and a recent bank statement from my father's estate, showing both my family name and married name, I am able to convince the consulate that I really am an Ellingson after all. I get a new passport, and immigration is finally satisfied on *that* point.

Now they tell us that Santiago must have a legitimate business to show he can support his surely-to-be expensive North American wife. We are once again stalled, dead in the water. We have no such business. Between what he makes doing odd jobs, and my savings, we are making ends meet, but that isn't good enough for immigration. What now?

Around the same time, I am ill, *very* ill. I have been ill enough times to realize I need purified water all the time. There is no regular source available outside Merida. Although there is one small plant in a village 40 minutes away, the supply is highly irregular.

We find a place in Merida that sells small filters to purify our house tap water. Small filters will be sufficient because we don't need much purification. Our water comes from rain which we collect in a PVC tubing system off the roof. We store the rainwater in a huge, below-ground, covered cistern.

Within a week of starting the rain water purification system, word gets around the village, and I have a line of people coming to the house asking for purified water. Then the schools come, and the health clinic, and then the personnel from the nearby Mayan ruins, all seeking a close source of purified water.

Within two weeks we have changed our order twice for a larger production system. The gods are helping me again. We now have the business we need to get married and a means to support us in the future. So what if I know nothing about reverse osmosis? I have a Bachelor of Science degree. I have had chemistry and physics. I can read. We can do this.

Within a few more weeks, we have a water purification plant that has the capacity to produce 1,500 gallons a day. We have to set up the chemical kit to test for bacteria and water hardness in the master bathroom as it is the only room with enough space. It also has a lock on the door to prevent small, curious children from possible accidents.

The large 5,000 liter PVC water holding tank, for both rain water collected from the roof and occasional village water, is built on the outside terrace, just outside the master-bath window. This drains into the small room below where the reverse osmosis equipment and water-softening tank needed to produce the purified water goes. To have any privacy at all when using the toilet or the tub, I have to add a curtain on the bathroom window.

In time, we have to add three rooms in a separate building next to this, extending behind the house. The first of these rooms becomes the filling station, the second room the bottle washing area, and the third room storage.

This building opens from the back, except for the filling station. There, Rose and I find ourselves filling all the bottles, from liter to five-gallon size, with purified water.

We have to create a road behind the main house to access this building by truck for loading and unloading. The building has a metal roof where the iguanas (*Hu'u* in Mayan) fight and play, always entertaining us.

The washing room attracts hundreds of butterflies because of the water. It is christened *Pe'epen*, butterfly. The orioles, the *Yuyas*, sit and sing their lovely songs in the *chaka* trees outside the filling station. These trees remind me of madronas, which grow in Oregon, with their peeling bark exposing their shiny, satiny, olive green skin below.

As it turns out, we will have this business for four years, employ half the family, and supply not only our village, but four others nearby as well as the various ruin sites in our area. It involves all the girls and two neighbor girls. I teach them "Business 101 and Accounting."

We learn that the little girls are the fastest to get apart the sticky labels we design, make, and must put on each bottle we sell to satisfy the state Health Department. But I learn I am the only one who can place the labels on straight. Brother Max is hopeless, but he is the best at cleaning the bottles. Rose and I become the fillers, as no one else likes to wear the necessary masks and gloves.

Santiago teaches cousin Doroteo to drive the truck. The both of them do the actual run—the delivery to the various places. Santiago is a natural salesman and our business grows.

We run seven days a week most of the time. At the same time, I juggle caring for the girls, attending school meetings, making uniforms for the school, sewing dresses, and cooking, plus the usual hoo-rahs of running a business and raising a family at the same time. Without Rose, I am overwhelmed and cannot get it all done. She becomes my salvation during this time.

My Mayan increases as we go. I learn to count, ask, "How many?" (*Jaipe'el*), "How much?" (*Bajux*), "Of what, of which?" (*Maákamak*) I learn that "*Jekin-tal-te'eló*," (I am here) is shortened to "*tal-te'eló*," and means the same as "Hello, anybody home?"

We also sell Popsicles and ice as demand dictates. The house is a constant stream of activity.

By early November, we have jumped through every hoop immigration has thrown at us. I have now changed my name back to my maiden name, learning at this time that women here in Mexico do not change their name upon marriage, and realizing how clever that is. We now have the required business.

We plan to marry in December when my son is free on vacation from the Academy to come down. My daughter is still in the Navy in the Persian Gulf and can't attend. We have received permission from the village registrar to have the ceremony performed at our house since I am not Catholic. We have the electricity bill receipt, in Santiago's name, showing our address, to prove we really own a home here.

I quickly learn that your electric bill receipt is your most important piece of identification in Mexico. Not your passport. Not your driver's license. Your electric bill: Never leave home without it. Not a copy. Keep the most recent original receipt in your wallet at all times. You are asked for it everywhere, all the time, to prove you exist here in Mexico.

As we leave immigration, papers in hand, having received permission to marry seventeen months after my arrival, amidst congratulations, *felicidades*, no one really believes we will stick it out.

The lady who has been working with us for months says, "By the way, the permit is only good for one month."

"*What!*"

"Yes, if you do not use it within the month, it expires and you begin the whole process again."

Scratch December. Scratch son being here. I can't believe it.

On Tuesday of the next week, I ask San, "When *should* we get married then?"

"Saturday," he replies.

"Which Saturday?" I ask.

"This Saturday." His other brothers who work out of town are free and will be home for the weekend. His friends are free. The registrar is available. It is all arranged. Really ...!

Women don't make decisions in this part of rural Mexico. Even though I have made hundreds of them by now, it never occurred to Santiago to ask my opinion about this. It has all been arranged. We have been given a list of things to buy in Merida—five kilos of this dried chili, six kilos of that one, chocolate, spices, sesame seeds, *ajonjoli*. I am learning dozens of new words again.

His women friends come on Thursday to begin the cooking. They make *molé*, a traditional meat dish that uses chocolate in the sauce, in the Zacatecan way, where the mother, Manuela, is originally from. This woman is like a second mother to him. He worked for the family and was raised with her children. Her daughter is to be one of our witnesses for the wedding. I do not know any of this, but it is all arranged. I am not to worry. There is nothing for me to do.

But, but, but ... clothes! What shall we wear? Invitations! Cake! What about those things? There is no time. We have to go to Merida tomorrow to get the dozens of kilos of chilies to make the *molé*. We have no time for this other nonsense. People will know. They will come. In the afternoon.

"Your black dress and white jacket will be fine," he tells me.

"And you?" I ask.

He shrugs. He has only one good pair of dark pants and one long sleeve shirt. It will do.

Lord, what *am* I doing!

"And your parents," I ask?

"They already know."

"The girls' dresses?"

"The ones you made for them will be fine," he says.

We have musicians I learn—the ones who play at the hotel where I stayed over the years. One of the trio is another cousin. They have been contracted to come and play.

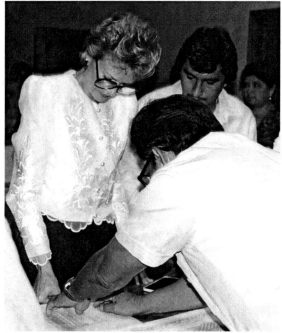

Fingerprinting.

And so, we are married on Saturday afternoon, where I learn that you sign and fingerprint about eight or nine pages of papers, as do your parents (in this case only his), as do your three witnesses. I did not know we had three witnesses!

I learn I am three years *older* than his "second mother." No one believes this, but there is my birthdate and year, followed by hers, on the document. She is one of our witnesses.

There is a cake, there is beer. Santiago and I have champagne, a good champagne that he bought unbeknownst to me in Merida. We are actually married and everyone cheers.

Signing papers.

I think I am in shock. The party begins, the food is fabulous. I have never had *molé* like this before. It has taken three days to prepare, this wonderful dish made with pork and turkey, chilies, chocolate, and sesame seeds.

The next day, another group of cousins and friends come back to help clean up the rubble. I am shooed away as they haul out the furniture, throw buckets of soap and water on the floor, literally hose it out, squeegee the rest away, replace the furniture, and "*ya, tzo-oki!*" (Already it is done.) We begin yet another phase of our life together in a clean house.

When it publicly becomes known we plan to have no child together—we each have two from previous marriages, and I have had a hysterectomy and therefore can have no more—the people feel very sad for us.

"We have enough," we say. "We are happy."

But they don't believe us. We need a baby.

I think I have quite enough on my hands as it is, but I learn that it is fairly common in the village for children to live with someone who is not their actual parent. It may be an aunt or older sister, but it can also just be someone who wants, or agrees to take the child. There is seldom an official process.

The happy couple.

Within several months, I am called on to go help a woman from the village. She is very ill. It is not uncommon for us to be called because we have one of the only cars in the village, and it must occasionally serve as an ambulance. The woman and her mother are well known to the family. I have made a couple of dresses for her two small girls. She has no husband, and there are several versions of why or where he is. I don't like gossip and ignore it all. The woman is bright, cheerful, and very talented at embroidery work. She has done many projects for me. I like her, so I go to see how I can help. Usually it is money and transport to a doctor that is needed. We have enough, and I am glad to help.

The woman is extremely ill. That much is obvious as I enter the door to the one-room, concrete sleeping house with a *palapa* thatch cooking hut behind it. She is very ill. I am at a loss as to what to do.

Most of the people in the village still believe in *brujas,* which are shamans or witches. I take many people to them—near and far away—over the years. I don't know what she will want me to do, but she at least speaks Spanish as well as Mayan. She is bleeding, hemorrhaging. Will she survive? What is wrong? She is pregnant. No husband. No money. Yes, I see the problem.

I get the shaman and the "things" she requests—a black chicken, some white cotton cloth, and an egg. I leave money with her mother. I can do no more. I leave.

A few days later, Santiago comes to me. She has survived. The baby has been born and she wants us to take it. Her family wants us to take it to give it a better life. But I can't do this. I am "too old" to start with a new baby. I now have three new daughters, plus Santiago's mother and ancient father, his sister Maria who is severely affected by constant epileptic seizures, a growing water purification business, beginners Spanish ... and *a baby*? Add in the fact that this child is of an unknown father. Gossip being what it is here, the child would eventually know who its real mother is. As an American, I cannot even entertain the idea.

I consider the ensuing consequences and I say, "No. I am sorry, but no."

The woman and her mother beg, they plead.

"You will give my child a chance," they say.

They break my heart in a million pieces but in my soul I know I can not do this. This is not best for the child. Not here in this village. No.

A baby we did not take.

The child is given to an older uncle and aunt who could never have children. I provide part of the money for its care. It is all I can do.

*   *   *

I see this now young girl from time to time, with her light brown hair and green eyes, like mine, and I wonder, "Was I wrong?"

It will be the first of three children we are offered. The last I will not know about until she is three years old. I would have taken her. I wasn't told this time because I had said "No" to the others.

Chapter Twelve
Some Things I Cannot Explain

The Maya here believe in many gods, superstitions, old legends, all mixed up with Catholicism. I grew up in a science, math, "logic and rules" type of family. Therefore, I am not really superstitious or very religious in a church-going manner. I have a great tendency to say, "Bah, humbug, that's hogwash" to things like pixies and leprechauns, fairies and ghosts, menehunes and Aluxes, or whatever you call the "little people." I do not believe in ghosts, although I know I have seen one. My grandmother, after she died was sitting in my front room, coming to "chat" and give me advice. I do not believe in curanderos, shamans, or witchdoctors *either, although I will question this in the future. So I cannot explain these next events, but they did happen.*

*   *   *

Shortly after moving into the house we built here, Santiago's uncle, *Tio* Pedro, dies after a protracted illness. During the final days, Santiago and I go down to be with the family, to offer some sort of comfort. One evening as I am sitting on the floor beside *Tio's* hammock, gently rocking it, he happens to open his eyes. Upon seeing me, he asks in Mayan if he is dead. Santiago says no, why does he think so?

"Because an angel is sitting in front of me," he says.

He is looking at me, whom he has never seen before, with my longish blond hair, green eyes, and white skin.

Later that night, after I have returned home to care for the girls, he dies at midnight ... a bad time to die. It is neither one day nor the next. The soul wanders around the village looking for other souls to take with it, so it doesn't have to journey alone.

The girls and I are at the house and don't know that *Tio* Pedro has died. We go to sleep. Shortly after falling asleep, a noise awakens me. I go to open the door from my room out onto the terrace ... but I don't. Something stops me. Now, the noise seems to be coming from the front of the house, so I go to the hall and through the house to the front door. Turning on the outside light and seeing nothing, I am again about to open the door when the noise moves yet again. It is at the back door now. Reversing, I go to that door, and as I am about to open it, Yuli calls from her room.

"What is the matter, what is the noise?" she asks.

"Nothing, nothing, probably a dog," but I know it isn't.

It had been brief footsteps, now gone again. I go back to my room and stand looking out the window for a time, wondering if I should go out and check. Something is stopping me, and it isn't fear. I am always wandering out at night when I can't sleep, watching fireflies, watching the bats sailing about, intrigued, not having had such things where I came from in Oregon. But this night, I do not open the door, I do not go outside.

Santiago comes running in shortly afterward, out of breath, asking "Did you open any door? Did you go out?"

"No."

"Did you hear any strange sounds?"

"Yes, like brief footsteps."

"But are you certain you never opened the door, not even to look?" he asks emphatically.

He knows my penchant for wandering about at night.

"No, I didn't open any doors, nor did the girls. Why?" Then he tells me of the belief that when a person dies at night, particularly at midnight, the soul wanders around for a couple of hours, looking for company, and can enter through any open door. No one ever leaves their doors open here at night, no matter how hot it gets, nor will they open one.

"Can't it get in through a window then also?" I wonder, thinking of the dozens of screened, louvered wood shutter windows we have, all open.

But none of our souls are taken that night. I didn't open the door.

*   *   *

I had heard many tales about the Aluxes, the little people that play tricks on you here and steal small shiny objects they are attracted to.

"Sort of like ravens?" I wondered.

I was advised not to build on this hill because the Aluxes live behind it, close to here.

"You will have problems," I was told.

But I didn't understand this with my poor Spanish and non-existent Mayan. I built anyway. Sure enough, small things began to disappear: paring knives, coins, a spoon, a metal key ring. Their hobbit hole must be full to the brim, I thought to myself.

*   *   *

One night as I am washing dishes, the girls drying, I hear someone calling outside, behind the house, and I suddenly leave. I walk out of the house and begin following "the voice," back through an old trail that winds into the hills. They say you can walk to Campeche on it. When next I am cognizant, I am fighting off Santiago, beating on him wildly, trying to escape. Escape to where, why? Where are we? We are on the trail, quite a ways from the house. As I slowly become aware of "reality" again, I wonder what I am doing here and why. Then I remember the voice, I can see in my mind's eye the place I was told to go. I ask if there is another hill close to here and a sort of tunnel—something like a chimney, that goes into the ground straight down, shaped like a bottle with a rounded bottom—off to one side of this trail?

Santiago ignores my question and leads me back to the house. It turns out that the girls had alerted him when I had suddenly stopped washing dishes and left. He came after me. I feel groggy, like I have been drugged by something. He leads me to bed and I sleep like the dead. But the next morning I can still see the "vision," the place where I am supposed to go. I persist with my questions. I won't give up because the vision won't go away.

Brother Max, the expert in these matters, is sent for. He listens and then tells me that I am describing where the *Aluxes* live. They are calling me. They can make trouble for me. I must find a way to appease them. This I don't believe. I don't buy it. But what happened, happened, so I ask to be taken to see this place for myself. Better yet, let me find it myself. Come with me, to see if I can find the place I see in my mind. They finally, reluctantly agree to accompany me. It is not a good thing to do, and they are afraid. But it is daytime and we set off.

After walking only a short distance, I can feel we are getting close. Soon there is the hill and, in the dip before it and to the right should be the "bottleneck" entrance. But I can't find anything. It is almost all grown over with thick bushes and shrubs. Suddenly, I almost fall into it, an opening about two feet wide. You can see down into it, but not far. It is dark below. They say not to go in, there may be snakes. But how far down does it go? I think, not far. In my mind I see a small room, like a cognac bottle.

We come back again later bringing flashlights and a rope to tie off to a tree and in we go, Santiago first. Max won't enter. Santiago says it is not too deep, so in I go. We are in the cognac bottle. But it is not all a natural formation. At some point it had been formed by man and a concrete-like covering put in place. It is called a *chultun*, a place to store water, perhaps a place to hide also. It is the home of the *Aluxes* now, but we find no paring knives, nor shiny objects—just bones, old bones of animals. Perhaps they fell in and died, not being able to escape back up the straight smooth wall of the bottle neck. We touch nothing and leave.

Max is adamant. I must find a way to appease the *Aluxes* or I will have problems.

I think about this for awhile, but nothing else unexpected happens. Perhaps they have gone away, perhaps it never happened. But I didn't imagine the hole.

Several weeks later, at dusk, I am up on the roof watching the fireflies as they make tiny twinkly Christmas lights all through the trees.

"Too bad you can't coordinate the fireflies' appearance with Christmas," I think.

Suddenly I feel a "presence," of something near, but nothing tangible.

"They have come to talk," I think.

I sit and explain to them that I mean no harm. I will not bother their home. I will protect it, keep it natural and wild if I can. It is land that has no owner, no use for crops, I will not cut the trees.

"Will that do?" I ask.

"Yes," I think, "it will."

"Perhaps I will try to buy it if I can, to safeguard it for you," I tell them.

*   *   *

Years later, I succeed in buying this land. I am leaving it natural, the way it was, just trails going through it. The Aluxes never give me problems again, nor do they sing the song of the sirens, calling to me. Did we make a pact? Max thinks so.

Chapter Thirteen
Seasons of Bugs

My mother used to ask me when I first came here, "What are your seasons like?"

I would think, "Cool and hot!"

We only have cool weather during four months—November, December, January, and February—when the Nortes come down from Canada and the eastern U.S. seaboard. They sweep across the Gulf of Mexico and whack the peninsula. The weather can go from A to Z in a day—from shorts to jeans and a sweater. You learn to enjoy the cool weather, store away those days to remember when it's hot enough to sizzle eggs on the concrete in April and May, when you feel like you are living in a blast furnace.

*   *   *

I think of the seasons and months by what insect or bird is prevalent. The *x kán ixi'in* come when the rain begins. You never see them during the day. They are attracted by the lights. Night falls, lights go on, and in a fierce year, hundreds of dark brown beetle-like creatures begin their siege, their blitzkrieg against the light source. They beat frantically against the screens, making a buzzing noise—like angry bees. They crawl under doors, enter through cracks or gaps in the screens, seeking the light. People simply shut the door, turn off the light, and go to bed early. You can see clouds of bugs zinging through the air around outside lights. The next morning, you sweep out dozens and dozens of dead or dying brown shelled bodies if you have left on an inside light. They crunch when you step on them.

My U.S. children first think they are cockroaches but they are not. And they are harmless. Unnerving, but harmless. You learn to push strips of towels or cloth under the door spaces when the *x kán ixi'in* come calling. In the years when the rains are scarce, there are few. Some years, it is a true barrage. This is when the rains are heavy and prolonged. They usually arrive at the end of May.

At the same time, and during the summer months, you find giant moon moths up in the corners of the ceiling. They come inside looking for protection against the coming rain storm. They are called *xma ha-nah* and tell you a hard rain is coming soon.

The ants tell you also. When the ants start marching four to six abreast, for miles it seems, you know a severe rain or storm is coming. They are the best hurricane alert. The ground seems to boil with them, marching in geometric lines, moving from one hidden den to another, cleaning and eating everything in their way.

I have seen the side of my house turn black, covered with them. I feared them at first, these big, angry, carnivorous ants they call *xulá*. But they seldom enter the actual house, although I have seen it happen, marching in lines down the hallway, following up and around door and window frames, following the tile patterns.

But they are just passing through—you and your house are in the way. They leave your house spotless, devouring all spiders and other insects, smaller ants, termites, everything in their way. Even big cockroaches cannot escape.

The ants swarm in trees and palms looking for food before a big storm, carrying it away to their underground bunkers, looking for provisions to last through the storm. Over time, I learn to accept them and to be fascinated and watchful of large troop movements. They are giving me information I should know, warning me of severe weather involving rain.

The Ani bird, called *chic-bul* here, eats them. If the trees are suddenly full of *chic-bul* birds—large, squat, dark, charcoal-colored birds with extremely short, stout, thick, curved beaks—look and you will see the ants' long lines moving into new territories.

I have stood at the mouth of their dens and watched the earth vomit streams of black ants. You leave them alone, for they have a nasty, vicious sting. But they are not after you. You are merely an obstacle in the road.

During March and April, when it feels like you are living in a corner of a blast furnace, the trees around our house fill with melodious blackbirds called *Pich* in Mayan. The air fills with a concert at full volume, the Pavarottis of songbirds.

When the rains come, late May to June through August and September, hundreds of frogs come into being overnight. They sing in the cisterns and water wells called *pilas*. They sit inside the PVC tubing drain pipes and call to their mates—the tubing echoing the voices of these small frogs. They climb in trees and chant from high perches. They can drive you quite mad if they are under your window.

They seem to have a magic signal around midnight that says, "That's it. Time's up," and they cease until the next evening.

In August and September, the tarantulas (*xchiwol* in Mayan, pronounced *sche wole*) move. They live in the base of the corn plant, the farmers tell me, and when they harvest the corn and disturb the roots, the tarantulas move elsewhere. We seldom find them around the house, as we are not near the fields, but if you are driving after dark you can see dozens of them crossing the highway between fields.

You watch where you step at night during this time. The tarantulas are impressive, big, hairy creatures. If you find one in or outside the house, you remove it with a long pole and then burn the beast. They tell me the hair from their bodies stings you. I prefer to smash it with a shoe.

The people also cut off just the stinger of the tail of the *alacrán*, the scorpion we have here. The village folk collect the body and bind this to a wart, believing it will dry it up. I have seen it work on two people.

We have snakes (*kan* in Mayan, pronounced, "khan") too, but not too many. We are coming back from the big water cistern one night after mending a malfunctioning pump, Santiago in the lead, niece Rose second, then me. There is moonlight and you can see very well. Suddenly, San and Rose both jump straight up and over six feet while screaming at me. But they are screaming in Mayan, and I do not understand. I look down and see a beautiful coral-and-black, thick-bodied snake coming at me. I was raised in eastern Oregon where we have rattlesnakes. In seconds, I determine that the snake is too close, and will pass slightly to the right of me. I freeze as solid as a stone, barely breathing. It is the way I was taught to react. After the snake passes, Santiago and Rose rush at me, pulling me towards the house, shrieking at me all the way. When we all settle down, I explain about rattlesnakes, and they try to teach me "The Flying Maya Two-Step."

One day I am driving to a neighboring village in the Volkswagen Bug. I have just come out of the last curve leading out of our village when I see an enormous iridescent copper-colored "rope" stretched across the road, the back forming a slight ridge, not round and smooth. I can neither see the head nor the tail. It doesn't begin or end. I slam on the brakes fearing that if I hit this monster, my car will shatter to bits. Heart pounding, I watch, entranced, as this huge creature slowly moves away into the bush, leaving the road free. Later that day Santiago tells me it was a kind of boa and would not hurt me.

I answer, "What does that matter if you are dead of a heart attack!"

Think of the insurance company, "*Señora*, how did you crunch up your car?"

I would say, "I hit a snake."

"Uh hum, of course, *como no, claro que si ...*"

We have fun creatures too, for example, butterflies that fight, sounding like tiny Samurai swordsmen, a toothpick battle, clicking and clacking away. They seem to have long, swallowtail-like wings. When the first serious rains come, hundreds of yellow and lime-green butterflies, *pe'epens*, swarm in clouds over the roads causing you to commit mayhem with your car as you smash into them. You cannot help it, they are everywhere. Why don't they stay off the roads? They gather around shallow water pools, folding their wings straight up, looking exactly like fallen leaves. The children pick small branches and bat at them. It is their spring game as soon as there is no wind for their plastic bag *papagayos*. I leave shallow pools of water around the house hoping to protect a few and because I love to watch them, so still and silent, like leaf statues. If you move through them, they swarm on you, turning you into a living butterfly perch.

We have gnats too. I think they exist everywhere. They can get through any kind of screen, they are so tiny. You learn to shut off the light and go to bed. They don't bite, they are just the messenger—enough for tonight, go to bed, tomorrow is another day.

Chapter Fourteen
El K'ooche

Now, as I write this, the K'ooche is starting. I can hear the music drifting up from the village, smell the chilies roasting, making me sneeze and my eyes run. I should be telling you about the K'ooche.

Rituals may be disappearing all over the world, but we still have them here. While they might be noisy, I think rituals are to be cherished.

*   *   *

I wake up, flying out of bed ... really ... at 4:30 a.m. on the second Monday of January to giant *voladores* (think big loud rockets) going off and a band playing somewhere in the village. The first year I hear this, I honestly think that maybe Guatemala has invaded us. It is also cool to cold, from our point of view during this time, so I wonder who is crazy enough to get out of bed at this hour. I also realize I can hear "*Cielito Lindo*" playing over and over by a very ambitious drummer, a trumpet, a clarinet, and a saxophone. Loudly. This wakes people up, and it is highly effective. It also signifies that they are ready to sacrifice the pig. The band goes playing through the streets to the house which will receive the saint for that year and be the statue's spiritual keeper, its host, for one year.

San Mateo is the patron saint of our village. The people believe that the statue of him came from the well in the village square. This is not actually a well, but has a tunnel-like entrance where you descend. The people believe that the tunnel once went all the way to the village of Mani (about 40 kilometers away), and that the Maya used it to escape the Spaniards during the Caste War. The tunnel is now blocked, but it did lead to an arched large room at one time. It may be that the statue was removed from the church and hidden in the tunnel by the priests during the Caste War to prevent it from being stolen or lost. Someone at some point re-entered the tunnel, found the old statue, and the "Miracle of San Mateo" began.

During a two-week festival time in January, beginning the second Monday—roughly the last two weeks of January—all hell breaks loose in the village. You hear the tunes of *"Cielito Lindo"* a million times, and strangely enough, "Oh My Darling Clementine." The people in the village set off ten tons of *voladores* rockets, and they haul the statue of El Santo Cristo de Amor in and out of the church almost every night. San Mateo only comes out once during this time, that being the final Saturday before the big blowout on the following Monday night. It is a hilarious, loony time with Catholic and Mayan rituals and beliefs all mixed together. This is quite an involved ceremony and must be done in a certain way.

Special foods are prepared for each day of the three-day cycle in which the receiving families are involved. Prior to this time, tons of a specific chili, called *yax-ik*, have been dried. The chilies are now burned to make a black sauce for the turkey dish they call *relleno negro*. Yes, *burned* chili— millions of them. It is literally a sort of stew made from ashes. Not one of my favorites, but they love it here.

When the villagers burn these chilies, clouds of invisible ash float through the air making anyone around suddenly begin to sneeze and cough fiercely, eyes watering. This means that someone close to you will be the receiving host that night.

The three-day cycle has someone starting and someone ending the ritual each day during the two week period. Fifteen different *socios*, or people in the group, receive the saint and prepare all the special food. To do so involves a huge amount of work, plus large pots, pans, and kettles, which the host families need to boil the pigs and turkeys, and make the *atole*, a ground corn drink. No one family can do all this work. No one family would have all the necessary items needed, such as the special knives and the work and preparation tables.

Therefore, many, many years ago they started a *K'ooche*, a procession to carry all the needed items in a big box, like a trunk, from one receiving house to the next. This gets carried on top of the much needed large work table with an inventory list of all the items.

Now this could have been done in a very quiet, casual manner, and once was done so, starting with the caretaker of the church. Years ago, one woman from each house passed along the necessary utensils and items. But that wasn't much fun, so something was necessary to wake the people up and get them going—slaughtering pigs, defeathering turkeys, and burning chilies ... something cheery at 4:30 a.m. on a cold morning, hence the musicians and the *voladores*.

This series of cycles goes on for 15 days—rising early each morning to get things started and carrying the items from one house to the next each afternoon. A little more diversion seemed called for, something big to look forward to. So the festive *K'ooche* was born.

Let's put four girls—related in some way to the receiving families—on a palanquin, a *K'ooche*. This was formed of the wood table, which was carried on poles on the shoulders of twelve to eighteen men. In days of old, this was also a means to carry infirm persons. To jazz it up for this celebration, the girls, dressed in their finest traditional gowns and seated on rickety, tiny wooden village-made chairs, carry the items from house to house at least once in this formal way during the 15-day celebration.

For further fun and games, each of the girls makes an offering to the guys carrying the palanquin, of a bottle of rum ... the cheap kind.

El K'ooche formal *terno* dresses, Rose second from the right.

So here we have four lovely young ladies—each dressed in white high heels and full ornate *ternos*, their hand-embroidered gowns with the embroidered underskirt, each layer edged in beautiful lace—being hauled, teeter-tottering, band playing full blast, through the village streets on the shoulders of some very to extremely drunk men. I have never yet seen it fail that somewhere along the route the girls are tumbled to the ground. I think it is an essential part of the *K'ooche*.

This formal *K'ooche*—with the girls participating—is only done on the last Friday. A symbolic key is passed from one girl at the last house to one of the girls of the next receiving house, along with the inventory list of the actual items.

The rest of the time, the items are taken from one family to the next any way they can be, accompanied only by the essential *voladores* and band.

Both Santo Cristo de Amor and San Mateo are honored here in the village during this time. Mainly this ceremony is to give thanks for the past good harvest and to ask for special care for the family members. There are two statues of Santo Cristo de Amor, so one is taken out of the church every night in a long candle-lit procession to the receiving house, while one is left in the church. The first statue is later returned to the church each day to be taken out again in the evening. But there is only one statue of San Mateo, so he is only taken out (and later returned) on the last Saturday before the whole celebration ends.

There is a *Rosario* of special prayers, which are performed in the church by a group of village women who know how these things should go. At about 9:00 p.m., another kind of celebration begins in the plaza at the base of the hill below the church. No one knows where this tradition comes from. It involves building a wood slat structure resembling a bull, a *toro*, covering it with ten billion firecrackers, and someone is convinced to *get inside* and "dance" while the participants light off all the firecrackers! Dance, he does, spinning wildly around the plaza and charging into the crowd. Firecrackers spiral out of control through the people, rockets and *voladores* going off overhead, some failing to be pointed upward and dive bombing the crowd. The people love it. Shrieking, screaming, and covering their heads, kids running crazy. It is a sight to behold.

The guy inside the *toro* has, as protection, a wet tee shirt and usually a *lot* of beer inside him. He always gets burned. Guys fight for this honor. There is never a lack of contestants. If the family receiving the saint has money that year, they may do three or four bulls the same night.

All this is being put on for the saint to see and enjoy. He has been carried out of the church to watch. They say the *voladores* are to make sure they have his attention. I say he knows what is coming and heads for Miami for a couple of weeks for a little peace and quiet!

After they have shot off all the *voladores*, 300 or more, and the *really* big rockets—the ones that send a shock wave through the air and sound like dynamite—and burned all the *toros*, the procession begins to take the saints statue to the host house. Everyone has a candle, and the length of the procession depends on how far away from the church the house is located. If the house is too close, they will circle around the village to make it last longer. Once at the receiving house, everyone who stays for the *novena* is given something to eat—coffee, *buñelos* (a kind of round donut), and crackers, something simple. The *novena* is a prayer session, pleading for good crops in the future and the safety of one's family.

Saturday is St. Mathew's Day—San Mateo. Because he is the patron saint of the village, he merits more than the usual dozens of *voladores*. More like a hundred will be shot off this last Saturday, from early morning until late at night. Regular ones that just go "bang" ... like a 22 rifle, to medium ones that make a sizzling sound in the air before going "Boom," to enormous ones that suck the air out and produce a tremendous "BLAM" that reverberates off the distant hills. All this is to honor San Mateo, poor man.

Dance of the Boar's Head.

Saturday afternoon also produces two dances—the Dance of the Pig's Head, which used to be done with a Jabali boar and now is substituted with a domestic pig's head, and the Dance of the Turkey's Head. Both these dances are performed by girls from the village in full formal dress, the *terno*, wearing every piece of jewelry the family owns, and using a special sombrero hat decorated with real flowers. It is a very elaborate, laborious affair. Two of our girls have participated in it.

Kindergarten children use a paper mache pig's head practicing the dance of the Boar's Head.

The actual dances are performed at the corners of intersecting streets throughout a specified route through the village. The procession can easily last a couple of hours.

To honor the pig, the girls carry long colored ribbons and weave them about, reminding me of a May Pole dance we used to do in grade school in the U.S., except the ribbons are attached to nails pounded in around the wooden structure holding the pig's head. Each girl chooses her "position" around the four corners of this table, there being approximately twelve girls involved in each of the two dances.

Tio Santiago imitating a woman at *El K'ooche*. Uncle Santiago: Age? As far as we can guess he was 75 plus years in this photo.

The third "actor" in this pageant is a man dressed up as a woman. He dances in and out among the two groups, telling tales and making people laugh. This is usually a wild affair that the whole village turns out for. Few outsiders ever see or are even aware of this celebration.

Today, no one actually knows why these dances are done, but it is logical to think that it is to honor the pig and the turkey, the essential elements of the Maya's special food dishes and so much a part of their life and survival. Pigs and turkeys are the Mayas' savings accounts, literal piggy banks. It is a rare village family that doesn't have them somewhere around their thatched cooking house or small concrete-block sleeping house.

The last Sunday in January, both the saints—San Mateo and Santo Cristo de Amor (the latter being the grown up Jesus versus the baby Jesus)—are taken out of the church. Every member of the hosting houses, every *socio*, fifteen in all, brings out their *estandarte*, their official huge highly decorated banner. These are surprising to see in these tiny villages. They are highly prized and guarded from year to year. The banners presumably arrived with the Spaniards and represent European customs, now mixed in with the Mayan. The Catholic priest officiates at this ceremony and in the procession that follows, as it slowly winds its way out of the church and through the village, the priest offering prayers at each corner, the whole ceremony lasting hours.

This whole ritual celebration culminates in a three day, back to back series of dances with huge professional bands beginning about 10:00 p.m. each night, really rolling by midnight, and ending in a grand ear-shattering finale at 4:00 a.m. Relatives show up from miles around, filling the town, and people come back from wherever they are working just for these two weeks. Combine two weeks of 4th of July fireworks, Chinese New Year, Easter Holy week in Greece, and you might come close to the effect.

Chapter Fifteen
Curanderos

The next time I am to come up against something I cannot explain it is a shamanic experience, a curandero.

*   *   *

I burn my left hand with grease splatters while cooking. Being distracted by the girls, I have not paid attention. I have four large burn blisters on the back of my fingers and thumb. I put the normal burn ointment on the blisters and think nothing more about it.

A couple of days later we go to a wedding, and one of my small nephews sits on my lap, repeatedly touching my hand, concerned because it must hurt. It does. What I don't know is that nephew Miguel has impetigo, a very common infection down here. In a few days, I recognize that my hand has become infected, whereupon we go to a local doctor.

It gets much worse and begins to swell, eventually to the size of a baseball glove. My skin is stretched so tightly that I think it will pop ... and hope it does. The pain is excruciating. Another doctor says it is herpes of the hand and predicts dire things, but the cure the doctors suggest makes no sense at all. Along with this, I am becoming ill in other ways. Food repels me, the very idea of it making me vomit. My head hurts, and I have a temperature. The pain from my hand becomes so intense that I cannot tolerate it and plead with Santiago to cut it, lance it, to get out the pus and poison.

He finally seeks out Brothers Max and Antonio who agree it must be done. They go to find a hermetically pure thorn of some local tree, very long and sharp. With Santiago and niece Rose holding me still, the brothers lance it, cutting a sharp line across the three fingers and thumb at the knuckle. I remember little else except the pain and a medicinal herbal brew they put on it afterwards, which they repeatedly reapply.

The swelling goes down, but I have gotten much worse in other ways. I can keep no food down, and my temperature is soaring. I am in and out of consciousness. The local doctor, Santiago's cousin Luis, comes and goes, but it is beyond his ability. He can do nothing.

"Take her to Merida," he says, but I am too ill, Merida is too far, and I know no doctors there yet.

I finally become conscious for a long enough time to realize that Carmen, Santiago's mother, is constantly in the room, clucking around like a hen, truly upset over something. She has come up from her thatch house below, concerned by what Santiago has told her. I look to where she keeps pointing and saying something in Mayan, in an agitated tone, to Santiago. And then I see it—a thin red line, creeping up my arm, following the vein from my infected hand. Blood poisoning. I know what it is.

Funny what your mind does. I want to laugh. Here I am. I have been warned against the poisonous snakes, the scorpions, and the tarantulas, the food and the water ... but blood poisoning? Never. My head hurts so bad, my teeth are chattering with cold from my high temperature, and the thin red line keeps creeping up my arm. I am to die of blood poisoning in the Yucatan jungle, from a grease burn and a wedding—a wedding where small, infected, concerned hands give me an almost lethal injection of systemic blood poisoning. I pass out again. It is too much.

I awake, smelling and looking like an old moldy spinach salad. Hovering about me I see Carmen, Rose, and someone I don't know, covering my hand and arm with this dreadful cold salad concoction, changing it each time it warms up, which is often. My arm is strapped to a board. I can't move it. And there is a thin piece of red cloth, like red flannel, tied around my arm, just below my armpit.

"What is the red cloth for?" I finally ask.

The red line has crept to above my elbow, getting closer to my heart, but I can't connect the thought.

I am told that the red cloth is to attract the red line. The red line will become confused by the red cloth and follow it, round and round, finally getting dizzy and going back down again. It can't pass the red cloth.

"Yeah, right. Round and round and round it goes. Where it stops, nobody knows."

I fall asleep again.

I do not know it, but the three of them, Carmen, Rose, and Santiago, continually change this herbal salad around the clock for two days. I wake up feeling better, for the first time in more than two weeks. The red line did indeed reach the red cloth—that much I remember—wondering vaguely where they would put me in the tiny cemetery. Would they throw my bones over the back wall in five years? Or just put them in a beer box, like they put the bones they have to dig up out of the cemetery when a new grave is dug. Now the line is back below my elbow, clearly receding. How? How is this happening?

Within days, I am well enough to sit up, but not to stand or walk. I feel terribly thin. They are making me drink some dreadful concoction they call *suero*, a glucose-type liquid. The only one I can keep down is apple suero, the others are too awful. I want a bath, so Santiago carries me to the bathroom where I chance to look in the mirror. I almost die of shock! I am the color of lemons, old ugly lemons, even my eyes. I look at my nails and they are a weird color too. My whole body is this color. "Yellow jaundice" is the only thing that comes to mind. My urine is very dark and smells. Something is still seriously wrong, and I finally agree to go to Merida.

In Merida we check into a tourist hotel where they have an English speaking doctor. While we are waiting in our room, we order something to eat. The doctor enters and instantly I have his attention. He doesn't ask any questions except who else has been in the room. He calls room service and gives specific instructions. The room is quarantined. He calls the hospital, where he intends to take me immediately, and orders tests. Then he notices my hand and the cuts across my knuckles. Santiago explains in Spanish, because I am too tired. The doctor calls the hospital back and orders more tests.

I don't remember much of it. Tests, needles, waiting, "Does this hurt, does that hurt?" More tests, more blood drawn.

I am now punched full of holes. My soul is going to leak out and dribble on the floor, probably an icky yellow color. It will probably stain their floor. I want to go home. Finally we are allowed to leave. We spend the night in the hotel, but no one approaches us and everything is plastic, or plastic covered—like airline trays of food.

The doctor finally returns with the results of two days of tests. What I have had, both occurring at once, is hepatitis and blood poisoning—septicemia. The doctor can't believe I am alive and cannot believe that he finds no damage to the liver or other organs. I need no further treatment other than slow recovery and perhaps vitamins to help. *But*, everyone in my household must be instantly inoculated against hepatitis. Everyone.

Santiago and I look at each other and I laugh.

"Doctor, these people have been treating me round the clock for weeks now, they don't need it."

The doctor's protests do no good. As Santiago says, he grew up eating dirt. It can't poison him. Any weak one would have died of such things years ago. I am the weak one.

I begin to wonder, "Will I survive this country?"

*   *   *

Do I now believe in witch doctors, curanderos? *I can't say. Over the years I have seen scorpions tails collected and saved, brewed and bound over warts—and the warts disappeared. Black scorpions are best, they say. I have heard, but not seen, cures where you, the "afflicted," take an egg from your house, and a black and white chicken, a white cloth, and sometimes other things to the* curandero. *The two favored* curanderos, *depending on your problem, whether it is a "curse" set upon you by another person or an illness, are more than an hour away. We have taken many people to both, but I have never been witness to the entire ritual. But each time, out of the egg you have brought, comes a needle, a scorpion, or a bit of bone. This then helps determine your "cure," what you must do, which herbs or powders will be used, and if you will need to return and when. I have seen it work and not work. Epilepsy with gran mal seizures is a tough nut to cure.*

Do I believe it? I don't know, but I am still here and not in the cemetery.

Chapter Sixteen
Death and Dying in a Mayan Village

*I realize I am wasting time. Stalling. I have fixed a cup of tea.
I have cut a fabulous yellow tulipane, hibiscus to me, and floated
it in a small dish with salmon peach bouganvilla.*

*I am afraid to write this chapter, afraid of the memories it
will bring back. But it is pushing to come out. Like giving birth to
a baby, you cannot stop the process.*

*Bodies are buried in 24 hours here, not sooner. They must be
given time to be sure they are really dead. Not longer because of
the heat and lack of "funeral services." Relatives who could
possibly get here within that time are notified by almost
mystical ways. Verbal messages are sent with taxi and bus
drivers. The tom-toms are beating.*

*In the U.S., we are protected, insulated from death. People
die in hospitals, car crashes, sudden heart attacks at work, or in
hospice houses. We are shocked, saddened, and upset. But we
are rarely more than a small part of the process. Oh, we may be
there when it happens, but then the body is quietly whisked
away. There is usually a funeral or ceremonial service of some
sort. Some religious person speaks of the dead in a church or
synagogue and the body is buried or cremated.*

I was not prepared for death here.

*   *   *

The first death I experience shocks me because it
happens so suddenly to someone I have known for some
years, a young man from the hotel where I always stay in

Uxmal. He was the cashier in the restaurant and was killed when he hit a field tractor while going to work on his motorcycle, his head almost cut off. The tractor had no lights. Tractors are never on the road at night, but this one had engine trouble in the field and was late going home. The tractor had just come over a rise in the highway just before the hotel where it could not have been seen in either direction. It wasn't even the man's turn to work. He had taken the shift for another man. It should never have happened.

They are very fatalistic here. When it is your turn to go, you go. You can't escape it. Maybe that's why they live life so casually and yet so intensely. Who knows when death will come?

Santiago's father comes to the house to tell us that the man who died was a cousin. They are speaking in Mayan, but I know it is death. They both are crying. The doctor comes later ... he is another cousin ... to sedate Ma Carmen, Santiago's mother. The doctor has performed the "autopsy" on a flat rock in the cemetery. Autopsies are mandatory here but there is no place to do them. We have no village ambulance to take the body anywhere else.

Santiago leaves with his father *a comprar*, which means in Spanish "to buy." To buy? Buy what? A coffin? I have never seen one here. Instead, measurements are taken to the village carpenter who, in the next few hours, will make a pinewood box to fit the body. It looks like a packing crate, the lid ready to be nailed on. The body is wrapped in a white cloth, clothed in a white shirt if possible, if it is a man. Then the box is placed on four chairs in the middle of the sleeping house where a vigil is maintained for the next 24 hours. The body is never left alone. It is cleansed, bathed, dressed, and placed in the box by the family. Candles in glass jars are lit and placed under the coffin and on the one table the family owns or borrows.

If a person is in the final stages of dying, from old age or illness, 11 candles for the 11 virgins—no one seems to know quite who they all are—are placed at one end of the room, stuck on the floor, lit, and burned only once until they burn out. The one table the family owns becomes an altar, with crosses and flowers, and more candles. The dead person's possessions—hammock, sandals, and clothes—are placed under the table with live oak leaves, called *hojas de roble*. As the oak leaves wither and "die," they pull out the bad spirits from the possessions. After eight days, the items can be used again or given away. They will be cleansed of any bad spirits.

When the 24 hours of the vigil are up, provided this is not at night, the burial is held. The box is carried in a procession through the village from the house to the cemetery on the shoulders of family men and friends. It is usually four men who carry it. Friends and family, walking with the coffin and ahead of it, make up this procession. When you see a procession like this, someone always says *"alguien compró su boleto,"* in Spanish, "someone bought his ticket." Every woman carries flowers from her garden. The female family members are supported by other female family members and friends.

While the 24-hour vigil is going on and the box being built, men are hired to dig a hole in the cemetery, directed by male family members. There is little rhyme or reason as to where the grave is dug. It is wherever space is available.

The village people refuse to enlarge the cemetery as they believe that then more people will die.

After five years, the old plots are dug up and the bones removed, hopefully to a small metal box to be placed in small concrete shrines. Sadly, I have seen peoples' bones laying in old cardboard liquor or beer boxes, labeled who it was. Often there is not enough money to buy the small metal box.

One day, I find Santiago's uncle's bones. He died just after I got here. I had taken Ma Carmen to place flowers on a family grave, and there are his bones piled in a beer box, the skull on top staring at me. "Pedro Dominguez," a hand painted sign says. I am so appalled. I come home demanding to know why his bones are just sitting there in the middle of the concrete slab section of the cemetery in a beer box! No money. I promptly go to the next larger village where they have metal boxes and buy one for his bones.

The actual interment involves simply lowering the box by rope into the hole. The hole is invariably the wrong size and digging begins again. Women are now hysterical and collapsing. There is no "service," no priest. Someone speaks in Mayan, sometimes they sing, and then they begin to fill in the hole. Mothers, daughters, and wives try to throw themselves into the hole and have to be physically restrained. Then people begin to filter out. The first stage is over.

Next, for eight days, a *Rosario* is to be held. A *resadora*, a woman who knows the old songs and procedures, is contracted to come and sing special songs, pleading permission for the departing soul to be admitted into "heaven." The table still serves as the altar, adorned with flowers, white candles, crosses, and special food. A chicken is killed and prepared with black beans that are cooked and ground fine, pureed. The food can be eaten after the prayer session ends and the spirit of the dead fed. The *Rosarios* can last for hours.

In the first year of death, this ceremony is repeated at the one month, then the sixth month, and finally at the yearly anniversary of death. This must be done for each person who has died in the family if they observe the traditional Mayan way. My mother-in-law Carmen is traditional. Flowers from the garden must also be placed on the grave at each of these times.

Chapter Seventeen
The Face of Life

You cannot be sheltered here. From a small child on, you are involved in life—birth, death, family problems, crop failure—reality—day-to-day life. No one is "protected" from seeing these things or hearing about them as we are in the United States. It is assumed that a child is fairly self-reliant. Thus, children are present at every occasion. They witness birth, death, family problems, and attend fiestas ... with the same self-calm. It is a natural progression of life here in the village.

Most births occur in the home, aided by a midwife, a partera. *There are few hospitals in the region. Lack of money and trust keep people from going to them. Childbearing is natural and most comfortable in the home, with all the women you love around you, supporting you, instead of strangers in masks that you have never seen. The men are not excluded, but truthfully prefer to stay outside, doing "something," or going to work as usual. Birthing, after all, is women's work.*

The only exceptions are emergencies, when it all goes wrong.

*   *   *

Yolanda and her husband Doroteo, Santiago's cousin who works for us as a driver in the water purification business, are expecting their second child, having lost the first one early on. No one is expecting any problems with this second baby. Yolanda is going for a routine check-up towards the end of her pregnancy. Because Doroteo is driving for us that day, I am asked to take Yolanda to her appointment. We set off, she and her mother-in-law, *suegra*, sitting in the back with me as the driver. The *suegra* always goes with the young wife who now belongs to her mother-in-law. They always sit in back, together.

Half-way between here and Ticul, a matter of only a few kilometers, Yolanda suddenly rolls her head back and passes out. I see it in the rearview mirror. I race for the clinic, demand my way in, and soon have a doctor, thank God. He takes one look at her, takes her blood pressure, issues frantic orders to a nurse, and jumps in my car.

"How fast you drive?" he asks me in fair English.

I reply, "As fast as you want."

"Go!" he says, "Fast you can."

"What about *topes*?" There are many between Ticul and Oxkutzcab, the location of the regional hospital. The topes will slow me down considerably.

He replies that the highway is being redone and there are none right now. I make it to Oxkutzcab in about 10 minutes. The doctor is frantic, afraid that Yolanda will die before we get there.

Thankfully, she doesn't. Alberto Antonio, whom they always call *José Miel*, honey bee, is born by Caesarean section, as are her next two. All three are normal. All three are our godchildren, that is, godchildren to Santiago, Rose, and me.

Vicky is Yolanda's second child, her real name being Veronica, who will turn 15 this year. We will all be expected to play a major part in her *Quince Años*, her fifteenth birthday coming of age party, as *padrinos* and *madrinas*. Whenever a godchild sees you on the street, or in passing, they say *"Buenas dias, Madrina,"* or *"Buenas tardes, Padrino,"* no matter what age. The third and last child is Luis Angel, with a true face of an angel, but the personality of perhaps a fallen one.

Padrinos—left to right, sitting on the couch: Doroteo, Yolanda, baby Luis Angel, the author, Santiago, and Rose. Sitting on the floor: Veronica (Vicky) and Alberto Antonio.

I was here in June, starting construction on my house, when Gibran was born, the youngest of Rose and Mimi's brothers. Yuli and Mimi, still small then, delighted in taking care of him. This brand new baby was born the same summer Yuli came for the first time. Rose and Mimi's mother, Berta, popped out this baby so fast in her thatch hut it made your head swim. Suddenly there he was. It was her tenth, after all. Berta had lost one before, in the hospital, and was not going to repeat that experience. Home was better.

Birth and death—every Mayan child understood it—as I had not. I stood outside a hospital window in Prairie City,

Oregon, when I was almost eight, to see my new baby sister, held up in front of a window by a nurse. I was not allowed to see my mother for 10 days, much less witness the process or hold a brand new baby.

I got to hold Gibran, and it scared the heck out of me. He felt younger and more "raw" than my own babies when I finally got to see and hold them. I remember being so afraid with my first full-term pregnancy, having had a very difficult birth, feeling abandoned, in terrible pain, with no woman I knew beside me, utterly alone. How I envied these women here. They had so much support. All the women they knew and loved were beside them during difficult times. How I wished they could have been with me.

I saw women nursing their babies every day of my life when I got here—everywhere—even in Merida, even at fairly formal occasions where the modern would mix with the old, village women still preferring their formal *huipils* over anything else. The *huipil* is made with a large square neck line, cut fairly low front and back, making it easy to pull the neckline down and expose the breast for nursing.

Breastfeeding was not a question in my generation. It simply was not an option. And I am sad for that. I missed a chance. I cannot imagine how it must feel, seeing and feeling life being given to your own child.

Here in the village, breast feeding was simply the way it was. You bared your breast and fed your baby, anywhere and everywhere—weddings, baptisms, *Quince Años*, or afternoon visits. It was the norm. No one hesitated, no one was embarrassed.

No one used plastic diapers either. Many times small children ran around their yards with no panties at all, just squatting down when necessity hit them. Our neighbor Lucy says that not until her daughter, now 15, was born, did it become popular to use *Kleen Bebe* Pampers. Money coming in from the north made this possible somewhat, allowing women that small privilege. It is also when bottles came into use. Before then, I never saw a bottle, much less a pacifier.

*　　*　　*

Breastfeeding is still a way of life for many women. No money from the U.S., or new concrete houses, will change how these women nourish their children. They do it because they want to.

Chapter Eighteen
Traffic Accidents and Mexican Law

I have seen much of death here, but this one stays vivid in my mind, the scene seared into my brain forever. It also came close to sending Santiago to jail.

*   *   *

I have just gotten out of the bath, hair wet and dripping, when I hear my niece Rose, who lives with us, come running, screaming, into the house.

"*Momi*! *Momi*!"

Rose is the calmest person I know. She is never hysterical, and she never calls me "*Momi*." She and Santiago had gone in the truck to bring home long poles that the men have cut up in the jungle, poles they need for the *corrida*, the bull fighting ring they are building in the village. She is still screaming and frantic.

I yell, "I am upstairs," while throwing on clothes.

She rushes in the door, covered with blood, babbling in Spanish and Mayan—something about a wreck, someone dead, I must come, *now*!

I freeze as I realize Santiago is not with her.

I ask, "Where is *Tío* San?"

"Gone, he is gone!"

Oh God, I can't breathe. But I must. I have to be calm. I ask, "Who is dead?" not wanting to know.

"An old man." She is saying she has to wash and change her clothes, and we must *go*!

"Wait Rose. Slow down. Tell me what has happened."

She tells me that a tourist bus hit the back left side of our truck when trying to pass it while going uphill into a curve, barely missing an oncoming car. The bus then clipped the left front side of our truck while pulling in front of it to avoid a head-on collision with the other car, flipping our truck over twice. Our truck came to rest on the cab, killing the old man riding in back that we had given a ride to, who had been coming in from his out-of-town fields.

The accident occurred just past a tourist Mayan ruin site. One of the guards at the site, who has a car, had raced here to the village for the doctor, bringing my niece with him. I am told to bring a sheet, a towel, something white, and money. I grab a white towel and all the money I have as we race out the door. Rose and I roar out in the VW bug. The accident is not far.

Santiago and the doctor are just getting into the doctor's car as we arrive. They are in a hurry and speaking so fast in Spanish I can barely understand them. But Santiago looks okay, nothing broken. He is shouting something about the bus, hiding, someone will let me know. He grabs the money, saying I must stay with the body, and then they fly off. I am stunned.

I finally see the body, the head smashed like a pumpkin, blood and brains leaking out the back, turning the pavement dark. The legs are still trapped under the truck and under the poles. I don't even know who the dead man is, but I do. I realize the towel must be to cover the head, protect it from the blazing sun. I am not prepared for this. Rose is shaking, she is in shock. I cover the man's head, and we move away and sit down, my arms around her. We are holding each other.

Soon a man from the ruins brings us water. Then Antonio and Max show up, pedaling fast on their prehistoric bicycles. These are two of Santiago's brothers, one is Rose's father. He takes Rose and Max takes me. Max puts his baseball hat on my head, to cover my wild hair and protect me from the fierce sun.

I ask him who the old man is, and why we are waiting, for whom? I am horrified to learn the old man is one of three brothers, my favorite little old men in the village, that I see going to and coming from their fields almost every day. I learn we are waiting for the police who will blame Santiago for the accident if they can't catch the bus driver before he abandons the bus and flees. That is where San and the doctor have gone—to try to catch the bus. It is a tourist bus and they know the route. I will have to deal with the police.

Santiago will have to hide until we can get an *amparo*, a sort of legal protection to keep him out of jail while we file a demand against the bus driver and his company. That is why Santiago needed the money. My head is spinning. I have no idea what to do, what they are talking about.

I learn I must go back to the village later and offer to pay for the coffin box for the old man, to buy the animal crackers, coffee, and rum to offer to the family, so as not to offend them. Even though Santiago was only trying to do a favor for the old man by giving him a ride, still I must do this, and then be part of the all-night vigil if the family will allow it. I am not prepared for this either.

I have no idea how I get through the next week. How is it that Santiago and Rose, wearing no seatbelts, were unhurt when the truck cab was smashed almost flat, rolled twice, and the windows all smashed to bits?

After reassuring the girls, I set about doing the things I am told to do. Someone comes the second day with a secret message to tell me where Santiago is. I can finally see for myself that he is really all right.

They find the bus, abandoned at a restaurant near Uxmal, where the driver has left all the tourists stranded. After months of haggling, the bus company finally pays us 10,000 pesos, one-sixth of the cost of the truck. There is no insurance. The truck is totaled, but Santiago and Rose are alive.

*   *   *

What did those tourists think, seeing our truck flipping over, then being abandoned, stranded, the bus driver fleeing?

Chapter Nineteen
Don Indal

Don Indal at the beach, fishermen in the background.

Death can also come in other ways. Long, drawn out ways. With no hospitals, drugs, nor hospice houses. That is the way it came to Papí, *Santiago's father.*

"Don Indalecio" or "Don Indal" as he was called, was not a robust man when I met him, around his 83rd birthday. He died three months before his 90th. He shared his birthday, May 5th, with his grandson Miguel. I made them a big birthday cake one

year—his 85th and Miguel's 5th. Between them, they couldn't blow out all the candles, even though we only put on one for each five years. That's still eighteen candles. We think of May 5th as "Cinco de Mayo" in the U.S. with lots of tequila parties in Mexican restaurants. They had never heard of such a thing. It is the Battle of Puebla in reality and not a very special holiday here on the Peninsula, but it was their birthday. It was a special day to us.

Don Indal and Miguel's birthday celebration.

* * *

When I first buy the truck, about a month after I decide to stay here and not go to Portugal after all, *Papí* is horrified to see me drive. I go back and forth to the next larger village alone, where the small hotel we are living in is located, while the house is being built. *Papí* worries incessantly, especially if I am late returning in the afternoon. I shouldn't be driving alone, not driving at all really. Women do not drive down here outside the large cities and few drive there either.

One day I return later than usual. *Papí* is standing out by the street, leaning on his cane, hand shielding his almost blind eyes, scanning the road for the truck. I stop the truck beside him. He asks why I am so late. I reply without thinking, that some drunks had stopped me on the way into the village to jabber—convinced they could somehow speak English that day.

"Where?" he asks me.

"By Amalio's house," I reply.

"Who were they?"

"I don't know. They did no harm."

Papí marches off, and I park the truck. Several minutes later, out comes Santiago, Brothers Max and Antonio, plus *Papí*. They are quite upset. I am asked to describe the men, which I do, and they race off, leaving *Papí* to guide me—*take* me—inside the cooking house. I don't understand what is going on, and *Papí* will answer none of my questions. No one else speaks Spanish—the women speak only Mayan—and the women are silent, suddenly busy cooking.

In a short time, the men are back with the two drunks that stopped me. It looks like a hanging party. I am frantic to explain that they did me no harm. No they did not touch me. No they did not insult me. The men finally let the drunks go, but I never forget the episode. There are different rules down here.

One day *Papí* wants to go to the beach, to Celestun, so we build two wooden benches to fit on the sides of the truck bed in back, so the whole family can go. *Papí* and Ma Carmen ride in the front with me, with Santiago behind to pound on the cab, indicating turn right or left, or stop. We have at least twelve people riding in the truck, and we are way overloaded. I drive very carefully. I have grown up driving pickup trucks.

We spend the day at the beach, the women wading out in the water in their white embroidered *huipils*, the girls and men in their long pants, laughing and playing. Someone buys fresh fried fish from a vendor, and we eat it with our fingers, washing off in the sea afterwards. We muddle along to several beaches and rent a launch to go see the flamingos in the river estuary that flows into the sea. I take a wonderful, wonderful photo of Don Indal that day. He is sitting in his one good pure white shirt and pants in the sand, woven Panama style hat on his head, leaning on his simply-carved horse-head cane, staring out to sea. Cataracts have almost taken his vision. What does he see? Does he know it will be his last trip to the beach?

Carmen in the water—*huipil* and all, from left, Mimi, Carmen, San, and Yuli.

Papi's health goes slowly downhill over the next six years until he can no longer get about, can't see, and can't hear well. During his last month of life, he is in the hammock the whole time, in the sleeping house below, where he wants to be. His friends come and sit and tell long tales about their childhood, all the things they used to do. The best storyteller is Don Santiago Arana, my husband's namesake, *tocayo*, as they call it here. Don Santiago makes everyone howl with laughter with his jokes and tales. He used to dress up every year as a woman for one of the ceremonial dances, which calls for a man to impersonate a woman. There used to be four men who did it, then two, then only him. We know we will lose Don Santiago too, but for now, he keeps us all sane.

We never leave Don Indal alone that last month. Sister Maria, his daughter, died six months before of a long continued series of epileptic seizures that couldn't be stopped, in the same hut, right beside him. I don't think he really understands she is gone. This is terribly hard on Carmen, mother and wife, losing both so close together. Her other daughter Pilar is there continuously, along with Rose, Santiago, and me. The girls, Mimi and Yulisley, are in school and still have to be cared for too. We take turns cooking, washing clothing, bathing, and changing *Papí*, thin as a stick. We rotate two by two, staying with him and Carmen during the night. Sometimes he hallucinates, thinking I am a young Carmen, jabbering away, wanting to be rocked in the hammock, to be held. I sit in a low chair at the side of the hammock and rock him, hold him, listen to him, assure him we are all there. Santiago sleeps with him at times, but he is so frail, like a dried-up, dead leaf, that we are afraid we will break him. It is February and cold sometimes. We are all exhausted and go down one-by-one with the same cold/pneumonia that soon takes Don Indal.

I think it is the hardest thing I have ever done in my life, watching him slowly slip away.

He goes on a night when I am not there ... but I know. The women start crying and sobbing. Carmen is worn out and hysterical. We sedate her and take her up to the big house to sleep. Then we set about cleaning and washing the husk, the shell that has been Don Indalecio Dominguez—*Papí.* There is no one to help us. No undertaker, no funeral home. Santiago has to go get the box made, the hole dug, the friends and family notified. His brothers are all out of town working, except for Max.

Max was Indal's stepson from Carmen's first husband who dropped dead in the fields at a very young age, years ago. Don Indal was 20 years older than Carmen, but he needed a wife and she needed a husband for her first three children. Don Indal was Santiago's father and Santiago was the closest to him.

When *Papí* dies, Santiago and I meet on the trail between our house and the hut where he died. We stand with our arms around each other and cry. But we know we have to go on. There are things we must do. There are animal crackers and coffee to buy. The vigil will be in our house, not someone else's.

Next thing I know I am not standing in a corner watching this. I am *doing* this. Washing and clothing a dead body. The eyes won't stay closed, neither will the mouth. Is the soul trying to get out? We are all emotional and physical wrecks. It has been too long, this dying. My own soul feels like it has been shattered into shards. I am *not* prepared for this.

My own father died at the age of sixty-three. I thought I would die too. My first father–in–law died years later, a death too long and hard. I loved him very much. But there were hospitals, closed caskets, and a cremation urn. This is here, right in front of me.

I cannot say, "Sorry, I can't do this."

There are not enough hands and arms without mine added in too. And so I do it.

We begin the long vigil. We talk. We welcome people. We make coffee and serve animal crackers. The next afternoon is the burial. Not quite 24 hours.

I take Carmen in the car, with her daughter Pilar. Carmen is too weak to walk. All the relatives are there. Food must be fixed for them too. A thousand things we must still do. Where are the girls? My mind flits from thing to thing. Carmen collapses at the cemetery, and the doctor tells me to take her home, and the little girls. I am glad to go.

*　　*　　*

It will take us weeks to recover in spirit and body. Carmen now lives with us. We will celebrate the fifth-year Rosario *soon. It is February again. I have already bought the candles. A neighbor has given her a special white and black rooster to sacrifice. Maybe Carmen won't cry this year.*

Chapter Twenty
Things You Learn,
Skills You Use

Growing up in the lumber camp.

It is not that odd that I end up here and am happy in this village of around 1,500 people. It's like stepping back in time 40 years. They say there are around 4,000 people here, but that is baloney. Three-quarters of the men and boys over eighteen work out of the village in the U.S., Merida, or Cancun, and are seldom if ever home. So let's call it around 1,500 inhabitants, with a maximum of 2,000. It's a damn metropolis compared to where I started life in Unity, a sawmill camp in eastern Oregon. That camp town still exists, but the sawmill does not. My younger sister and I were raised in this tiny town for my first six years. We left shortly before my seventh birthday to move to the "huge" town of John Day so I could attend school. John Day had 1,555 people. I think back then they counted people's grandmothers ... and cats and dogs too.

Eastern Oregon, logging country.

The sawmill camp had, besides the mill, our house, the office next door, a red cottage where my grandparents came to stay at times, the repair shop across the mill lot, and an old trailer house where Jonah lived. They said Jonah was a kind of witch, had mystic powers, they said. I liked him. He once gave me a great big doll that I had forever. Next to him was a tiny house where Art and Golee lived. Golee made the best pickles in the world. I loved to go to her house, especially when there was a card game going on. Golee smoked and drank with the best of them, and I thought she was swell. On the other side of the highway there were about four mill houses and the cookhouse. Alberta and George lived in one of these houses. They were like second parents to me. Alberta taught me "manners" consisting mostly of "ladies don't do that, Kristine," (in her eastern Oregon twang), and how to use a chamber pot when it was too cold and dark to go to the outhouse. Thankfully *our* house had an inside bathroom.

The sawmill in Unity, Oregon.

Up in the town itself there was a saloon called, "The Watering Hole," a post office, the U.S. Forest Service building, a grange hall where they had dances and meetings, and two grocery stores with a gas pump out front of each, one across the road from the other. Strattons and DeMeyers. I think it depended on which way you were going, where you'd stop. They were both the same. A one room, high ceilinged, if–you–can–find–it, you–can–buy–it kind of store. Just like those here in the village. There was also a church, the white pointy-spire kind, where the Reverend Pickthorne officiated. He used to flap around in a big black sort of raincoat affair, skinny as a scarecrow. I thought he was the devil himself. I sure didn't like him.

Our house was right by the log pond where they would dump the logs. Guys would jump on these floating logs and use a pole to move them towards the moving meshed-tooth log shoot that ran into the pond. They used a barbed pole to do this, and once in the mouth of the shoot, the mesh would catch the bark and drag the log into the sawmill to be sawn up into boards. It was here that I learned to swear so well. The men had a language all their own, especially when it was cold and they fell into the pond. You heard some great things then. It was better than pulling the heads off my mother's flowers, which she didn't like at all. I got my mouth washed out with soap a lot though, learning the language of the "pond monkeys." That's what they were called, pond monkeys. Agile as heck, jumping from log to log. The men who built my house in Yucatan brought that memory to mind as they clamored around on their flimsy pole and 2 by 12 scaffolding, raising the concrete block walls of my house. They swore beautifully too.

The lumber camp, our house in the middle along with the office buildings. Repair shop is far right.

Since I was the only kid until my sister came along two years later ... and a girl at that ... I had to learn the rules of the world of men. There weren't too many, but if you wanted to be where the action was, with the men, you had to learn these rules well.

The sawmill camp in winter with the wigwam burner on the left.

1) You do not fidget. Men hate fidgeters. If you don't fidget, they forget about you.
2) You do not get hungry or thirsty, unless they say you can.
3) You don't cough at cigar smoke.
4) You never have to go to the bathroom. Men have different equipment and there usually isn't a bathroom anyway, at least not one you'd want to use.
5) Always take some *small* something to do or play with. It can't make any noise or get in the way. A book is good. Men can talk for a long time and you might get bored.
6) And last, don't *ever* whine. Men hate whiners 'bout more than anything.

If you knew these rules, you could go in the office anytime you wanted. You could learn some great things there, but "You never tell nobody what you heard. Never."

These rules have served me well down here in Yucatan. At church weddings, baptisms, school meetings, waiting in the bank, waiting in the hardware store, waiting in government offices. Waiting. It's the same.

One of my favorite places growing up, besides the office, was the mill itself. I loved to sit on the sawyer's lap as he sat on a moving platform that raced back and forth. He was gauging how many boards he could cut out of each log and watching for hidden knots that could flip the log up in the air. He was watching this huge saw make boards out of a tree. I loved the smell of the pine. I hated it years later when it all got mechanical. Push a button and the log calculated, flipped, and sawed all by itself.

The town girl "cowgirls." I am the oldest.

When we moved to a larger town, we all got horses. Just about everybody rode, at least on the hill where we lived. We were in 4-H, we went to the rodeos, we rode in parades, we practiced "stake and barrel," along with "thread the needle," on horseback, just like everyone else. You needed to know how to ride bareback using just a hay rope for a bridle or you weren't "in." I have pictures of the four of us sisters (we were four by now), lined up like stair steps in our rodeo outfits—jeans, boots, cowboy hats, pearl snap-button cowboy shirts. Amazingly, it was Dad who took us shopping at Farrells every year at rodeo time. Pretty spiffy, we were. Not as good as the *real* cowgirls, of course. They lived on ranches. We were just town girls so we had to learn sewing and cooking, "manners," junk like that.

We also grew up learning to drive a stick shift, none of this automatic business. First it was the old Willy's Jeep with the choke button on the floor, later the big Chevy pick-up with four gears. You couldn't use the emergency brake on a hill either. That was cheating, unless it was a *real* emergency. You killed the engine when Dad told you to and started it again without rolling back or adios trying for your driver's license. Our mother made us practice parking between barrels in the empty lot next to the house until we could do it in our sleep. She gave us about a five-inch tolerance on either end, six inches max from the imaginary curb, and it had to be straight as an arrow. And we had to do it in one shot. Back in, pull forward. That's it. None of this jockeying back and forth. Try doing that in a mammoth '63 Buick station wagon!

*   *   *

These childhood skills serve me well down here, as I demonstrate to Santiago on the hilly San Francisco-like cobblestone streets of Zacatecas and Tlaxcala in the interior part of the country. I know exactly how wide my car is and the power needed for passing buses on the narrow, winding roads that are the norm in Yucatan. And I teach Santiago everything I know. He has always lived on the mostly flat Yucatan Peninsula and has had no need to learn to drive on hairpin mountain roads. This skill comes slowly to him as we travel up through Chiapas and Oaxaca and down around Mexico City through Orizaba to Catemaco. These are sinuous narrow mountain roads, cloud laden, where he learns about black ice too ... almost too late. Not too much ice driving in the Yucatan!

All of which is why it was ridiculous that Papí used to worry incessantly about me driving alone between here and the next larger village, a mere 15 kilometers away. But then, he didn't know any of this about me.

Women don't drive here outside the cities, especially not a standard stick shift, and not in this village. But I do.

Chapter Twenty-one
Growing Pains

After you have been here for quite some time, you begin to realize how much you have changed, and sometimes at what cost that change has come. It is never easy to go live in a foreign country, especially in a very rural area. City folks have their way of doing things and country folk have theirs. Spanish is not the first language here, it is Mayan. Many school meetings and ejido (farmers) meetings are in that language. It isn't their problem if you don't understand. It is the same with the land, the food, the dress, even the way you shop for food. The people have their ways, and you'd best adapt.

*   *   *

You find that much of what you know doesn't work well here. You don't clean the tile floor grout by sliding around on lime halves in the United States. You don't go to the store and pick out filet mignon by pointing to which part of the recently dead butchered cow hanging in front of you, you want. You find there are at least six to seven kinds of avocados when you thought there was only Haas. You didn't know they could make corn ice-cream, nor grind oatmeal in the blender to make a drink called *Cebada*. And yes, they really *burn* the chilies to make the all time favorite special occasion dish called *Chili Relleno Negro*. Ash stew with turkey, as one woman put it. Doesn't mean you have to *like* it.

You also realize that you don't need eight pair of pants or fifteen pairs of shoes. One or two, or maybe three will do. You have to hand wash it all anyway, so why have so much? You will be considered lucky if you have one jacket or sweater. So why *did* you have so many clothes before?

At some point, you start comparing your present life with your past one and you realize that you are actually happier *without* all that "stuff." The phone doesn't ring incessantly nor the TV blare all the time. You've left the material world largely behind.

Santiago had an interesting observation after a trip to the United States. He said that it didn't seem that most people talked to each other much. Here, it is about all people do. Sit and chat after all the chores have been done. Everybody. Old folks, little kids, sisters, friends. I didn't know I missed that until I found it again.

I *know* my husband. I am with him every day. He drops a kiss on my head or the back of my neck when he passes by. Our nieces and the girls who work on staff, as well as the yard man and boys, all say *"Buenos dias"* every morning, as does everyone. It's the custom here, and a nice one. It's a gentler way of life, but life here can also be intimidating.

The accident with the truck was a good harsh lesson. The law is not as you knew it, and you *better* know it, especially as a foreigner. You do *not* have freedom of speech as you might think. You will be judged guilty until you can prove yourself innocent. And it is still very much a man's world, and women would be well advised to remember that.

I had an identity crisis between my second and third years here, and it was quite difficult to surmount. Without Santiago's help, I doubt that I could have. He was gentle and kind and patient, and helped me to understand why I was having this crisis.

In my past life, I had been Eric and Clair's Mom, Kris Clark jewelry designer, Sig's daughter, a wife, and a daughter-in-law. I had a place, a niche, and now suddenly I had none. Everything I thought I was, was gone. Things that I thought I knew and were important were either worthless, not impressive, or wrong. College degrees don't count here unless you are a lawyer or a doctor. They didn't like my kind of jewelry design.

Plants wouldn't grow, but I was planting the wrong thing in the wrong way. This land doesn't want to grow snow peas or English cucumbers. It doesn't even like zucchini! Zucchini turns into round balls and barely survives! Whoever heard of such a thing?

Dwarf marigolds grew waist high and had a blossom the size of a dime. Ditto for broccoli. Who knew there were five kinds of limes, each with a very specific use. Lemons won't grow. Instead there is a large tree with tiny cherry tomato-sized orange fruits that taste just like lemons. So how many of those would it take to make a lemon pie?

You look for baking soda in the pharmacy or in the cleaning products part of a large grocery store. Baking powder is known by the brand name, Royal. Who knew that *bics*, Vicks Vapor Rub, was good for any insect bite or bee sting? We thought it was for colds.

You could find the best peaches and strawberries at the gas station. Truckers would come down from central

Mexico bringing flats of the fruit and berries when in season and sell them at the gas stations as they passed through. If you were there at the right time, you scored.

I came down with what can only be called "inappropriate clothing." I brought silk and linen ... to a village. They all got recycled. You would be amazed at how long those clothes lasted. Years later I would see someone feeding the pigs and chickens wearing the skirt half of one of my silk dresses, cut off and remade. A dusty grey-green fur grew on my leather shoes from mold.

Sometimes my attitude and sense of "what's right" was just plain incorrect. So maybe you don't know what's best all the time, maybe your way isn't right for living in a Mayan village, and you take a long hard look at yourself. You may not always like what you see, but you can also get some happy surprises.

*   *   *

You have to look for clues as to who you really are. What used to be rather dubious abilities in the past might now be useful skills. Instead of hiding some of the things you know how to do, you can be free to use and exhibit them.

You get comfortable with yourself.

Chapter Twenty-two
La Corrida

Years later I thought that maybe the village accepted me, kept me around, for entertainment purposes. I remember when I was watching the men building the house, laboriously cutting the boards to make various concrete forms, with an old saw blade rigged through a frame of bent steel rebar. No one had a drill pistol either. On our next trip to Merida, I bought a drill, various sized bits, and a small skill saw, all of which I knew how to use. I proceeded to plug in the saw and show them how much faster and easier it was to cut boards this way and even cut various angles.

Santiago's father was horrified, certain I would cut my hand or arm off. Not with a father like mine, you wouldn't. He owned a sawmill and had four girls, so he just taught us how to do all the "boy stuff" anyway—run a chain saw, buck up wood, split kindling, work outboard motors, use drill presses, work a two-man cross-cut saw, change flat tires.

Now, give me a machete, and I am completely helpless. With a machete I could cut my leg off, unlike the girls here who wield them as handily as I would a chain saw. It depends on your training.

*   *   *

Over the years, I continue to shock the people here, put nicely, with the things I can do. But nobody knows I can ride a horse. This is not horse country like some parts of the Peninsula.

However, every year in April, the *corrida* begins here in the village. These are the local bullfights. Funny, corny ones, not the least bit formal or professional. It's a five-day diversion from everyday life with almost mandatory attendance by everyone. Old ladies, small children, all the men, all the young people, EVERYONE goes to the *corrida*.

The *corrida* begins with building the corral ring itself. This is built by a group of men, an association, with each man being responsible for building and charging admittance for his section. Since brother Max is one of the *socios*, associates, we have ringside seats.

The corral is handmade in sections out of poles harvested from the nearby jungle.
Photo courtesy Nidia Alvarado

Over the course of two to three days, each man (and his brothers and friends) go out into the hills and cut poles to build their section—the whole thing being a beehive of male activity and beer. A hodge-podge of poles, planks for the chair seating section, thatch roofing on at least part of the arena anyway, all come together section by section to form an arena of sorts. The low rent district, the cheap seats, are at ground level, separated from the actual bull and horse-riders by a latticework of thin poles. Not much protection there, but that's part of the thrill.

The second level is reached by climbing a pole ladder (don't be wearing a skirt here!) at the back of each guy's section, where you find tiny chairs crammed together and a front part where you sit, legs dangling down into the arena itself. You need to be able to pull your legs up quickly if you choose this area. You are exactly at horn level. The *vaqueros*, the cowboys, come from the surrounding area, and so do the bulls that mostly stand around wondering how they got into this mess. I have yet to see more than a few actually charge anything or anyone, but there is always the hope it will happen. The *torero* (I am being generous with the term "bullfighter" here) mostly stands around nervously flapping a piece of red cloth at the bull and runs like hell for the nearest wood shield to hide behind at the slightest movement of the poor bewildered beastie bull.

The "cheap seats" are at ground level behind the latticework. Photo courtesy Nidia Alvarado

The *corrida* begins at about four o'clock in the afternoon and lasts, amidst the dirt and the dust and intense April heat, until 7:00 p.m. It can start earlier, and it can go longer. Towards the end, after some 50,000 *caguamas* (quart sized bottles) of beer have been drunk, someone is sure to jump (or fall) into the ring to prove how brave he is. Mostly though, it's the cowboys' show. There are way too many of them crowded into the small ring, flinging their lassoes, trying to rope the bull's horns and drag it out of the ring. Any eastern Oregon small-town rodeo is more exciting than this, but the crowd loves it anyway.

You need to be able to quickly pull your legs up if you sit at horn level. Photo courtesy Nidia Alvarado

The horses in the Yucatan are mostly small and uninteresting to me, but occasionally you see a real beaut, a "Wow" of a horse—big, powerful, prancing, and snorting around. Then I wake up and take interest, which is what got me into trouble this time.

The horse is tremendous, especially for a horse down here. He moves beautifully and takes perfect commands. He looks like he can do a lot more than the rider is asking of him. Big brute of a cowboy too, using way too much power for what is needed for the horse.

I had a horse a little like that once. Big quarter horse, stubborn as a mule, needed a spade bit. He was a trained cow-cutting horse that could sit down on a dime—just sat on his haunches, boom. If you weren't prepared for it, you'd go zinging off into space, right over his head. My father didn't want me to have that horse, but I finally convinced him I could handle it. My sister was the horse rider, not me. I loved that horse—a big Strawberry Roan. This one is a roan too.

Typical cowboys, vaqueros, and their horses at La Corrida. Photo courtesy Nidia Alvarado

The *corrida* is winding up, and I have sent the girls on home with Grandma Carmen. I am waiting for Santiago, but he is off with his buddies gossiping—everyone comes home for the *corrida*—so I decide to leave. At that time, the *corrida* was held in the village plaza, five blocks from our house.

As I set off walking, the big roan comes out of the arena, and I say to the rider without thinking, "Nice horse," in Spanish. The *vaquero*, thinking I am just another tourist, says something insulting in Mayan, which I choose to ignore. I continue walking.

Suddenly the *vaquero* is being verbally accosted by several voices, belonging to ... my family. Brother Max's voice is unmistakable. It has a quality and timbre that you can hear for blocks, let alone yards. Max has overheard this insult. Max is my great buddy. We ironed out our differences years ago, and I have just been insulted. I turn around, and there is a phalanx of about seven men—family and friends—all well-tanked-up and determined to defend my honor.

I tell them, "Really, it's no problem, I'm headed home."

Not good enough. I am detained, Santiago is sought, the owner of the horse is dragged out of the cantina ... *now* what have I done?

This degenerates rapidly and an argument erupts.

"She can't ride this horse!" the vaquero says.

"I didn't ask to," I reply, "I just said that it was a beautiful horse!"

"Well you couldn't ride it!"

"I didn't *ask* to ride it!" I say.

As the old *vaquero* and I trade glares, Santiago intervenes. He starts talking to the owner in rapid Mayan, which I can't follow. People *had* been streaming out of the arena, going home. Now some are drawn back, there's some excitement here.

Santiago finally turns and asks me in his still broken English, "You can ride this big horse?"

He has only seen me ride once, in Belize, a trail ride which he barely survived. Horse rider, he is not.

I reply, "Yes, I can ride that horse, but what's the point?"

Santiago answers, "The owner says if I sign paper saying I not kill him if you dead, you can ride."

Oh great. I sigh and start to explain once again that I didn't ask to ride the horse. Then I see Max and Antonio's faces. This has become a challenge. It looks like family honor is at stake here, through my witless comment.

"All right, I'll ride the horse."

"You sure you can?" San asks.

"Yes."

By now, this horse is wired. He looks like one of those horses who would just love to take a chomp out of your rear as you mount. As the cowboy flings me the reins, I notice the spade roller bit—a spiked wheel in the bridle— inside the horse's mouth, which is used to control very spirited horses. It is not pleasant on the tongue. I wish myself a little bit of luck, tighten up the right rein so the horse can't take a chunk of my buns, and make a speedy mount. This is a big horse. Gotta be 16 hands, which means his back is slightly over my head standing on the ground.

Someone yells, "You can't ride like that!" meaning I have no jeans, boots, or chaps.

I have on Bermuda shorts and huarache sandals, which have thin leather soles and no heel. The person is right. My feet could slip straight through the stirrup—smooth leather on smooth leather. I kick off the huaraches and pitch them to Santiago—better to go barefoot.

The owner tells me I am limited to the corral/arena only.

Fine by me. So we enter.

People are now streaming back in.

My little nephew is calling, "*Tia, tia! Tia's* going to ride!"

He is wild with excitement.

The horse is responding well, but he is hyper and nervous, as am I, so we just canter around, checking to see which commands—foot, rein, and voice—he responds to. He changes leads beautifully, switching easily from one leg leading to the other. Stops perfectly, just like I thought. Sits right down on his butt. This is what you need when you have roped a calf and are scrambling off to flip it and tie its feet. The horse needs to keep that rope taut and may have to back up to do so. I vaguely wonder who trained this horse. By now, horse and I have forgotten the crowd and are having fun. We do some old parade, 4–H stuff— sidestepping and prancing. I wonder if he will back up. He does. I shorten the reins and put them around the huge Chiapan style pommel—big as a dinner plate—and signal to back up. I put my hands behind my back while the horse backs up across the arena.

The kids go nuts. This is better than the circus!

We better do a finale and end this. This horse wants to run, and so do I. We get as far as we possibly can on one side of the arena, and I get ready, lean suddenly forward, jab him with my bare heels, and he springs forward like a loaded juggernaut, going like thunder for the other side of the corral. Just as it looks as if we will crash through the other side, I pull back hard on the reins and he sits on a dime. What a great horse! We canter slowly back across the arena and drop to a walk. I dismount, hand the reins to the owner.

"*Gracias*," I say, "*muy amable*." Thanks, that was nice of you.

I walk towards home. It takes a block until I remember my sandals.

I don't know how much money is won off that little scene but the family is certainly happy. The owner of the horse comes the *following* year to ask Santiago if I am going to ride again. They have a horse that I *can't* ride this time, a real mean one. It turns out I'm meaner.

We ride for over an hour-and-a-half through the dirt streets of the village, flying like the wind, not restricted to the arena this time. They catch me at the end, leg swung over the saddle horn, drinking a Coke, reins on the ground, the horse standing perfectly still, my small nephew perched on front for a short ride. Such a mean horse!

*   *   *

That was the last time I rode down here. Enough was enough. The family honor was avenged. The village had been entertained. Another skill from my childhood had paid off.

Chapter Twenty-three
The Modern World
and "Old Farts"

We closed the water purification plant Kich Kalem Ha, *meaning "beautiful water" in Mayan, when Coca Cola rolled into town with five gallon water bottles on the truck as well as Coke. We knew we couldn't fight the big guys, so we remodeled the rooms of the plant to form the first four rooms of the tourist guest inn that we still have, "The Flycatcher Inn."*

Santiago works in his blacksmith shop on a wrought iron decoration, designed by the author, for one of the rooms at the Flycatcher Inn.

The following story was triggered by a recent breakfast conversation here at The Flycatcher Inn. Since it was not the first on this subject, I thought I would share it with all of you.

*   *   *

I would probably have to be considered in the "old farts" category now. This is a term that was popular when I was younger, used to describe people who were impossibly old—dinosaurs, "older than the hills," anyone past 50 and surely 61 qualifies. We girls were not allowed to use that particular term, but we heard it all the same.

As you know, I started life in the tiny sawmill community of Unity, Oregon. It was somewhat like here, but we had a real phone that worked there, way back when. Here, we are still awaiting a land line phone ... after 16 years.

The phone in Unity was a box that hung on the wall, with a sort of funnel affair that you spoke into. Another funnel, which you held to your ear, was attached to the wall box by a cord. I could only reach this by standing on a chair. It was a party line. Three rings was our line, while five rings was our neighbor's, and two shorts and a long was someone else's. It wasn't polite to interrupt another's conversation—unless it was an emergency—or to listen in. People did both.

I could always find my Dad by asking the operator, who knew where everyone was all the time.

"Oh hon, he just went by The Watering Hole, you'll catch him at the mill in a couple of minutes." Or, "He said he was going to Strattons'."

The Watering Hole was our one and only tavern and restaurant, and Strattons was one of two stores carrying everything under the sun from canned goods to fishing lures.

In our small town, the operator was kind of like a cell phone. She made sure somebody could always get a hold of you somewhere.

Later, in the slightly larger town of John Day, where we moved just before my seventh birthday, we got different phones. I met a guest here at our Inn who said that when they finally got a phone, her mother made them go and use the pay phone up the street because the home service was so expensive when it started. The phones at that time were the big old rotary dial ones, where you stuck your fingers in the dial holes and spun it all the way around for each number.

Our office manager in John Day was named John Brown. The phone number was "1." Try calling that from someplace like San Francisco or Hawaii! And it, of course, all had to go through the operator.

Our phone numbers were simple: 1, 93, and finally 646. Everyone was aghast at the ones with three digits, sure no one would ever remember them.

In time my sister and I would even get a phone of our own, because our Dad got tired of the line always being busy with our calls. We could then yack for hours with our favorite friends, but this wasn't until high school, in the mid- 60's. These phones were called "Princess phones," but they were still rotary. "Push button" phones had yet to be invented. Imagine that.

In Tacoma, Washington, where my grandmother lived, the phone numbers had names *and* numbers, like SKYline 9- 7279, or CHErry 4- 2408. Later these were converted to numbers only, and you had to learn it all over again. I remember when they added area codes and the numbers became impossibly long. Now, I look at cell phone numbers and international access codes, and I have to laugh. But nobody really remembers phone numbers anymore. They are all programmed in the phone and you just punch a button for the name. The phones are now so tiny, you can barely find them.

Ah yes, the dinosaur age we came from. Computers were unheard of. Did we even know the word?

My father had one of the first companies to get a "computer." This was a huge mainframe computer that took up most of a wall in a specially built room that was carpeted. It had special wall coverings, air conditioning, and you had to get permission to enter! Only one person was allowed to work with the computer.

So I grew up knowing nothing about computers, but my children did. Their uncle was one of the first people we ever knew to have his own computer. A huge Macintosh, as I recall, that nobody really knew how to use. It fascinated everyone but me. They would stew over this thing for hours every day, trying to learn how to work it. By the late 1980's, my kids were using computers all the time. Computers had become part of life but cell phones had not. That was still to come.

I was forced to learn something about computers in my former business. I soon hired a person to run my office, and, therefore, the computer. It was she who learned the skills, not me. I am completely computer illiterate. I manage to do e-mail and that's all. So how did my website get created? By my genius daughter-in-law, from far away. That's the beauty of computers and email, and scanning. All these new terms we have learned!

Computers are moving to rural Yucatan too. Little kids come into the e-mail place I use in Ticul. They know much more than I do! Kids have cell phones everywhere. We still have no land-line phone in our part of the village, consequently we have no e-mail yet on our computer. Cell phones now work all over the Peninsula and Mexico, but they didn't for a long time.

Guests have arrived at the inn and had a cell phone panic attack.

"No bars!" Referring to the signal strength bars on their cell phones. Or they would say, "No signal!" As though the world was ending.

We have seen people on the roof of the big church, pacing back and forth, trying for a signal. You can usually get one on the outermost, northwestern edge of our roof, but you can't move even an eyelash once you've gotten connected, or you'll lose the call. People often stop on the road on the top of the hill to Ticul and make cell phone calls!

It is only in the past year or so that service has become fairly reliable in this area of Mexico. I can call Hawaii. I called my daughter in Eugene, Oregon, and was so shocked when she answered, I didn't know what to say. I didn't think it would work.

When young people hear part of this story they look at me strangely, like I'm making it up. But I'm not. This is the world changing. Now kids are deprived if they don't have their own cell phones and are lost without them.

Santiago was born before the village had electricity, and he is only 45. It wasn't until he was around nine or ten that the village got it. Everyone was afraid to go out at night before the electricity, sure the spirits would get them. There was one man who used to walk through the lanes late at night, wearing big, squeaky, rubber galoshes, scaring people to death. Santiago's parents would never open the door of their small thatched house after dark. The doors all had small windows that you opened to peer out to see who was there.

Santiago also remembers when there was no road to nearby Ticul, the closest larger village to us, a mere 13 kilometers away. When it was time for him to graduate from sixth grade, his father took him to Ticul to get new shoes and six tiny photographs for the school certificate, proving completion of primary school. Everyone who graduated had to go to Ticul to get these six photos. They walked. The trail went all the way from the village, along where the road now is, climbing way up the hill, going over the very top. If you look, you can still see the old trail way up on the rock cliff that was formed when they blasted the road through.

When Santiago and his father finally arrived in Ticul, a trip that took about three hours, they would go to the market and split one *Torta*, a sandwich made with a tiny loaf of French bread, and one Coke. It was all they could afford. Then they walked home again.

There is a myth that says there is an animal, like a bull, that inhabits the very top of the hill, over which everyone had to pass. They called it *B'oob*. It comes out at dusk and eats all of you except your head, which it leaves. People were scared to death to cross this hill anywhere close to dusk, not to mention after dark. They were still afraid to cross this hill when I arrived in 1991, even in an enclosed vehicle.

*   *   *

My grandfather was born before men flew. He never did get on a plane. We flew a lot when I was growing up as we had a small private plane. Grandpa never got used to it. He would hold his breath and worry from the time we left John Day until we arrived outside of Tacoma.

My living down here would have been unthinkable to him. I can't even imagine what he would think about computers and cell phones.

But then, he was one of the old farts.

Chapter Twenty-four
The Great Road Trip

When you see a perfect hibiscus blossom, you should pick it. They only last one day. They open, are gorgeous for a short while, and then begin to wilt. So you should enjoy the perfect day this flower can give you. Some things in life are like that.

Such perfection can last an hour, a day, maybe even a few weeks—it doesn't last longer than that. We once had a perfect time with the girls.

When they were little, teaching the children how to use silverware in the dining room of the new house. From the left, Santiago's son, me (blinking or am I asleep?), Rose, Mimi, and Yulisley.

I didn't come down here to change people, nor to teach them my language and customs. I came to live among them and to absorb their way of life inasmuch as I could. But it hasn't quite happened that way. Things sneak in, things like different manners, and hygiene, and logic. I didn't realize I was teaching them a different way, but I was.

*   *   *

Quince Años—absolutely gorgeous! Janet, our neighbour.

Quince Años celebrations are big down here. Think of it as a "Sweet 16" birthday, only it's your 15th birthday. It's mandatory. Everyone does it, from the poorest family to the richest, and they spend every penny available to do so. They may have no food for the next week, and the kids may have no shoes, but that doesn't matter. *Everyone* has a *Quince Años*.

Birthdays are not my specialty. I would forget my own if I could. In the U.S., Grandma Jane always made the cakes for the birthdays. My first mother-in-law was a cake baker par excellence. I was not. I have had to learn to do this in Yucatan since there are no local bakeries that produce cakes, except for *tres leches*, a rather soggy affair, consisting of two layers of white cake and a cream-type filling. What is a birthday without a cake and candles? So over the years, I muddle through the cake-making process, managing relatively well to produce something edible for each birthday that comes along. But these are small family affairs with few or no presents. Gifts are not expected here, the families have no money for such frivolities ... *except* for the 15th birthday.

A *Quince Años* here is a true all-out bash. A new dress, fancier than a wedding dress, high heel shoes, gloves, hat, and a flower corsage are mandatory. You must have attendants, both boys (*chambelanes*) and girls (*damas*). The family pig, reserved for this occasion, is slaughtered, plus innumerable chickens and turkeys. All the older family women are contacted to help with the cooking preparations. Chairs are rounded up from everyone you know. No one ever has enough. If you order the beer from Superior, they also bring more plastic tables and chairs for the guests. Cases of beer and coke and other soft drinks, heavy on the *beer* side, must be bought also. A band or musicians must be hired.

This can run into thousands of pesos, and almost always turns into a drunken bash, ending at three o'clock in the morning, or whenever the beer runs out, leaving you with hangovers and mountains of garbage as souvenirs. I have been to enough of these to know that this is not what I want to do, not what I want for my two soon-to-be 15 year old daughters. Mimi turns 15 first, followed by Yulisley, a year-and-a-half later. So, I make a proposal. I give the girls time to think about it and decide what they wish to do.

Quinceañera walks through the village with attendants.

The girls have never been off the Yucatan Peninsula before. When I came, except for Yulisley, they had never even been out of the village, not even to the nearby archeological ruin sites. No one has the few pennies necessary to take the bus to a ruin site nor do they think it important enough to spend those pennies in this way.

I soon change that. We begin to take small day trips around the area. Later, when they have learned how to sleep in beds and not just hammocks, we make a couple of overnight trips. For the first overnight trip, we go to Merida for Carnival, which coincides with Mimi's 10th birthday. This is their first time in an elevator, eating in restaurants, watching TV until the wee hours of the morning ... and falling out of bed.

Over the years, we travel to Campeche, the old walled pirate gulf city on the Gulf of Mexico side of the Peninsula. We also stay several times at a small hotel near the huge lagoon of Bacalar where I teach them all to swim. We visit ruin sites, museums, and natural geologic formations such as cenotes as well as spring-fed, small, coastal lagoons. The trips are history, geography, and geology lessons all in one. I am both teacher and student, as we all learn together.

"Who does that statue represent?" I ask.

"*Benito Juárez,*" they tell me.

"Why was he important?" And so the lesson begins. I want to interest them in their own country and give them a reason to want to learn more.

My *Quince Años* proposal is simple. We take a major road trip, the five of us—Rose, Mimi, Yulisley, Santiago, and me. I know it will probably be the only opportunity to all travel together.

The year is 1997. Mimi turns 15 and asks to be called by her first name, Nidia. We all comply with this except for Grandmother Carmen. Santiago and I are "between careers," a kind of saying we have no job at the moment. However, we have enough money saved up to not be overly concerned just yet. We have a red Volkswagen Beetle named Ladybug. My proposal is to cram us all into it—luggage and all—and head into Mexico proper for as long as our allotted money will last.

The girls have never seen rivers, bridges, mountains, or waterfalls before. Our part of the Yucatan Peninsula has none of these beautiful things. I want them to see the huge suspension bridge over the Usumacinta River, the mountains of Chiapas, the archeological site of Palenque, the port city of Veracruz, and Lake Catemaco. I want them to steam in the heat of Villahermosa city, and to be bathed by the mist of the waterfall Egipantla. I want them to see El Tajin and the flying natives there called *voladores*, the museums of Jalapa, and the coffee and vanilla producing country—things that Santiago and I have yet to see too.

This is a difficult decision for the two girls, and I don't want to sway them. All of their friends are having, or have had, their big bash blowout *Quince Años*. I do not want them to regret, years later, not having had one. *They* have to make the decision.

We pour over maps and books, photos Santiago and I have taken on previous trips, and possible routes. We discuss the probable time we'd be gone (two weeks likely). In the end, the excitement of a trip wins. It is a "go." The only time we can do it is after year-end school exams but before school actually finishes. They are in secondary school now, the first people in the family to ever get this far in school. Both are excellent students. We got permission from the director to take them out of school for two weeks, the end of June and the first part of July, just before the real rainy season begins and when traveling prices are the least expensive.

Packing is not a problem for me, having spent years hauling my two U.S. kids all over the world as much as I could, but for these girls it is all new.

"One suitcase, girls, what you can carry, yes your backpack will be fine, and only clothes you can hand wash and that dry fast. Take a book—something to read—plus a deck of cards, nothing that will be upsetting if it is lost. We won't be going fancy here, so forget dresses. Remember your 'bathing suits'" (a novelty seldom seen on youngsters here).

Meanwhile I pack the survival bag—can opener, Handi Wipes, fork, knife, spoon, plate, plastic glass, detergent, clothes drying line, tuna fish, band aids, and sanitary pads (we are many girls here), quart-size plastic bags and garbage bags for wet bathing suits. Santiago is in charge of the car—tires, battery, fuses, jack, spare, everything.

Finally it is time, and we are off. Grandma Carmen is crying, sure she will never see us again. We will disappear into the maw of Mexico to be swallowed whole. There is still a working one-line village phone at one of the small grocery stores, and we promise to call. We have made arrangements for someone from the extended family to come every day to help Carmen, Indalesio, and Maria. Brother Max and Nephew Wilbur will stay in our house at night. Amid tears and kisses, we are off, headed for our Great Adventure, five of us crammed in the Volks, our "air conditioning" being the windows rolled down. It is about 35° Celsius or 95° Fahrenheit and will climb rapidly from there as we head up the Gulf, destination Villahermosa, about six to seven hours away.

The girls are singing. We have a tape cassette in the player, a mixed bag of everyone's musical likes, driver gets first choice. Santiago and I alternate driving. There are climbing flowering vines this time of year (late June), and the roadside is a blaze of fuchsia to lilac to purple. It couldn't be a more beautiful day. A "perfect hibiscus" day.

Taking a road trip in a small car with five grown people is not an easy undertaking. Add to it that the climate is hot and sticky, there is no air-conditioning, a lack of bathrooms (or most bathrooms in deplorable conditions), and few restaurants along the major highway routes. One crabby person can make the whole trip insufferable. This is part of the gamble we take, that we can all be good sports and get along. By and large, this works out to be true.

To arrive in Villahermosa by the inland route, you must cross a number of rivers, none more impressive than the Usumacinta, one of those "mighty rivers." If you have never seen a stream, let alone a grand river, this is a sight to see, especially because, in this case, you don't see it coming. You must first go through a toll booth and approach a slight hill. The next thing you see are dozens of wires and cables forming an inverted V, running up to two points in the sky. You are searching for the invisible hand holding these wires, pulling the bridge towards the sky. The design itself is simple, yet intricate, and it is a while before you notice ... *The River*.

I am wondering what they will do, what the girls will think. A river is not like a flat tropical ocean beach, especially not when you are suspended above it, like a bird.

Nidia suddenly says, "Yuli ... *mira!*"(look!)

Instantly, they are all goggle-eyed, staring at this immense body of water flowing beneath us. And then, we are on the other side.

Here there is a military checkpoint, common throughout this part of Mexico. While Santiago deals with the checkpoint, the girls are hanging over the back seat, still staring at the river behind us.

There is a turn-around spot just ahead, and I ask "Do you want to go over it again?"

"Yes!" comes the breathless answer.

And so we do, over and back twice, driving as slowly as possible, the military guard wondering what in the world we are doing.

The girls' first great river. They spot a ship, what they think is a tiny boat, and I tell them to keep watching it while we drive down to where it is so they can see the actual size, a huge tanker.

Silence follows for quite awhile, then comes the questions—"Where does the river come from, why doesn't it all flow into the sea, how can the ships go on it, how deep is it, why do metal ships float, how far can they go, why does the bridge stay up?" The lessons are beginning.

Villahermosa holds many things of interest, besides being maybe the hottest and stickiest place on the Gulf of Mexico. We lucked out and checked into a decent hotel in the center of the city, close to the river Grijalva, in a section that is closed to traffic. It has a pedestrian mall. As we walk around, what catches the girls' attention most are the elaborate bridal, bridesmaids, and formal gowns on display in the shop windows!

The Olmec outdoor museum of La Venta, with its enormous stone heads, is mandatory, as is the archeological museum, a river boat ride, and a trip through a maze-like jungle park.

We hit Veracruz in time for the *Dia de la Marina*, a day in honor of the marines. It includes an elaborate display of fireworks—a little more impressive than our loud boom, one-color-burst rockets in the village. We spend hours in the huge aquarium. Later at dinner in a tiny restaurant, we are taught how to make *Huachinango a la Veracruzana*, a fabulous fish dish, by the owner himself. Then we are on to Jalapa, in the hill country, in the mists, where they raise coffee and vanilla. We spend three days there, going through the incredible anthropology and natural history museum, the science and technology museum, and going in an earthquake simulator. We sample all the wonderful pastry shops in the old part of the city, losing ourselves in the labyrinth maze of tiny shops, trying on and buying, and laughing.

We come down from this higher elevation to spend several days in Catemaco, the lovely, small lake snuggled into the peaked hills along the coast, reminding me of Maui, Hawaii. Here we hire a launch and go through acres of water lilies and hidden rivers, winding between trees growing out of the water, going between islands in the lake, some covered with monkeys, and picking out where *we* would build a house. We see huge trees covered in beautiful white blossoms that up and fly away, the "blossoms" being white egrets. We walk up and down the narrow cobblestone and unpaved streets, buying strange fruits to eat. We enter the church to see their lovely Virgin, bits of paper pinned everywhere behind her, people pleading for miracles. She is said to work miracles to restore health. We hike into several waterfalls including Egipantla, where the girls stand in the mist and watch rainbows form in the air, laughing and shaking like puppy dogs from the cool wetness.

Catemaco, out on the lake.

The ruins of El Tajin, with the upturned-curved-roofed buildings make you think you might have awakened in Japan or China. El Tajin is close to Papantla, which is in the mountains close to the Gulf. It is the historical home of the Olmecs. Native Indian men climb an immense pole to a tiny square platform, ropes bound to their feet. Four of them fall away toward the earth, slowly spinning and revolving downward, upside down, their arms spread wide like giant condors. One stays on top continuing to dance, no safety ropes for him of any kind, dancing on a platform about 20 inches wide, 30 feet in the air. They call them *voladores*, the flyers. We stay and watch this twice—we are so entranced—and later talk with two of the "flyers." It is here the girls learn that they cannot understand the

Indian-Mayan-mix dialect spoken by the native women and children who approach us with their embroidered pieces to sell. The girls see embroidery designs they have never imagined before, so different from the ones that they know from our village.

We proceed to Palenque, the mystical ancient city in the low hills leading into the true mountains of Chiapas. Here we see an archeological site completely different than our Uxmal and marvel at Pakal's tomb, way down in the interior of the pyramid, dark and damp. We drive up to Agua Azule to find almost no one there but ourselves. Immense turquoise blue and green sets of cascade, after cascade, after cascade, flow down to form a large pool at the bottom of the gorge. We spend hours there playing in the water, feeling like we are the only ones left in the world.

Girls' vacation, 1997, Egiplanta, Veracruz.

We have been gone almost two weeks. We call Grandmother Carmen to tell her we are on our way home. She has never seen nor talked on a telephone before and almost drops the phone in shock when our voices came out of it. She keeps shaking her head, "Yes," and "No," in answer to our questions, too emotional to talk, not realizing we can't see her shaking her head. Nephew Wilbur finally gets on the line and tells us what she says and that everything is fine.

"Tell her we will be home soon," we say.

"She put her hands over her face and is crying," Wil replies.

You expect something to go wrong on a trip like this, and it does. The car hits a shiny slick spot in the middle of a blind curve on the Chiapas mountain as I am driving down from Agua Azule. The car spins in circles towards the cliff-edge in the on-coming lane. I pray no one is coming the other way, concentrating on everything I know to keep us from going over the edge. We don't, and I keep driving. No one screams, no one says a word, sound being frozen in our throats.

We next blow a tire suddenly in a narrow, hilly pass before Villahermosa, and the car veers out of control into the other lane once again, with Santiago driving this time. The girls learn how to change a tire.

The next morning the car does not start. We spend two more days than planned in Villahermosa as the car mechanics try to find out why the car isn't starting. They try everything *but* the ignition until I finally insist. But the attitude of all of us is calm and patient. We are on a road trip and having fun. How can you have a real adventure without at least a little danger mixed in?

We arrive home in time for the closing school ceremonies. Carmen weeps again with relief. Santiago is offered a job driving a truck for the power company putting up giant towers across the peninsula that eventually bring electrical power down from Chiapas. In the next six months, he is gone more than not.

The trip is the only one we will all make together and we will remember it forever. But for now, we are back in the land of reality—clothes to be washed, chores to be done, time to go to work again.

*   *   *

But the hook had been set, the girls' eyes and minds had been opened to something outside this tiny village, outside this flat peninsula. That had been my intention, and it had worked.

Years later I asked the girls, "What do you remember best of the last 11 years?" and they answered in unison, with no hesitation, "the trip!"

They dragged out all the old photos, and we relived every minute of it again.

Rose graduates from high school, her first year living with us.

The girls had always gotten along well together, all three of them. Rose was old enough—ten years older than her sister Nidia—to not compete with her, and Yuli was grateful for her new sisters. Rose was more like a younger sister to Santiago and a great help to me.

The "Jitterbug Babies," Yuli and Nidia (Mimi).

Yuli and Nidia were my jitterbug babies, they loved to dance and sing. I have a great photo of the two of them, jitterbugging wildly about the dining room, at one of our frequent impromptu dancing sessions. We all loved to dance. The two girls were close, "thicker than thieves," as my mother used to say, and this trip cemented us all together even closer, in ways we were yet to realize.

Chapter Twenty-five
The Inn Becomes a Funeral Parlor

Santiago's mother, Carmen, had two brothers still living when I arrived in Yucatan. The rest were deceased. One brother, Tio Pancho, lived in Chetumal, over on the Caribbean coast, and came to visit several times a year. We like him a lot. If you put glasses on Santiago and streak his hair with grey, you would have a duplicate of Tio Pancho. I know how Santiago will look as he grows older. Not a bad deal at all.

The other brother was "Don" Luciano, Luc for short, often called just Tio, uncle. For all the time I knew him, he was the caretaker of the doctor's pig farm, owned by the doctor and his brother Abram. As this farm is somewhat out of the village, we rarely saw Tio Luc.

*   *   *

Luciano is a curious fellow. He is not married. He is the only "self–invited guest" to every village event I have ever heard of. He goes to every wedding, *Quince Años*, and baptism, no matter who is giving it. He is rarely, if ever, actually invited. But he brings a small gift for each, beautifully wrapped, and goes anyway. He sits through the whole ceremony and fiesta, a big grin on his face. He enjoys these events immensely. How he finds out about them, no one really knows, but he is always there, and so everyone in the village knows him. He shows up magically at all our family get-togethers too—materializes out of thin air—just in time for the food. He never makes any trouble for anyone, nor helps with anything, but it is accepted that he will be there.

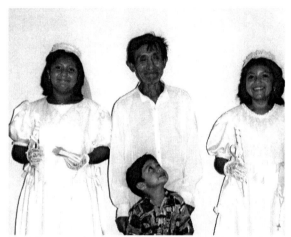

First Communion: From the left, Nidia, *Don* Luciano, Yuli, and in front, Santiago's son.

When he doesn't show up around Christmas time, we know something is wrong. This is the start of our third year with the Flycatcher Bed and Breakfast Inn that we have here in the village. Through good luck and hard work, it has become quite successful. This year, the third week of the Christmas-New Year period is jam-packed full, and we are turning people away. We have our hands full running the inn, with only one girl to help us. Our niece comes by when she has a couple hours free from the three jobs she is handling in local government politics.

Soon, word comes that Luciano has been taken ill out at the pig farm and has moved into town with a person we know. The next we hear, he has been admitted to the regional hospital with a severe respiratory problem and then taken to a hospital in Merida to attend him better. The problem is serious but not really surprising. Luciano does not take care of himself nor does he wish to live with anyone, and he has a bad penchant for lighting his cooking fires by burning old plastic bags. Not good for the lungs, but he can never be dissuaded. By the time we are able to arrange free time to go see him, word comes that he has died suddenly.

There are no funeral parlors or services here in the village. As I described earlier, the body is taken to the family home where all the rituals and vigils are conducted. For *Don* Luc this will be an all night vigil following his death in the early morning with burial the next day. Santiago's mother Carmen is his only sister. She has lived with us until recently when her arthritis became so bad that she could no longer navigate our hill and house stairs. Still, this is the family house. And so, it finally dawns on me that we are about to receive a body and become a funeral parlor ... with an inn full of foreign guests.

Niece Nidia comes flying up the drive on her bicycle with this news shortly after it has occurred to me. We look at each other in appalled silence. How are we going to pull this one off? Where is Harry Potter when I need him! We need a magic wand. Better yet, we need his magic "invisibility cloak" to make this whole afternoon, night, and next morning invisible to our guests.

The only conceivable place we can use for the "funeral parlor" is the original family sleeping *palapa* house down on the lower edge of the property. Carmen is staying with her son Antonio, here in the village. The sleeping hut is now in use as a storage area for Santiago's wrought iron supplies, metal projects, old cabinets, sewing machines, saws, and general *junk*. Mounds of it. This traditional pole house hasn't been used, or cleaned really, in over five years, since *Papí* died. Cora, our only help at the inn, is still here for the day, and so the three of us fly into action, knowing the body is due from Merida at any time. The question flits through my brain as to what the guests might think if they arrive back from a day at the archeological sites nearby at the same time as the body arrives ... but first things first.

We haul out junk, sweep, scrub, take down cobwebs, and begin to make the vigil area. The old stereo console, bought by someone long ago, and now crumbling apart, will have to serve as the coffee, hot chocolate, and food service space.

Someone is sent to see about a coffee server and cups, and to buy the needed food items. People and relatives are being notified by any means possible—cell phones, taxi drivers, and general gossip. We also have to be ready for the relatives who arrive for the all night vigil and next day burial, who will stream in at various hours of the night. They will crash on the temporary mattresses placed on the floor in the linen storage room and in hammocks hung every which way while we still try to do "business as usual." These relatives will also need food which will have to be paid for and prepared at yet another relative's house.

Finally we have the sleeping *palapa* house reasonably clean, the altar table ready, candles bought, flowers cut from the garden, a saint's image in place, but no white cloths. We need two white cloths to cover the table/altar and the coffee/food stereo console, and we have none. Everything is closed in the afternoon in Yucatan, and we need it now. I remember an old white embossed tablecloth we once used for Christmas. I scramble to locate it, hoping I haven't thrown it out or given it away, and that it is clean. I haven't and it is: one down. The tablecloth will cover the altar. Finally we sacrifice an older twin flat bed sheet, the only white one we have, for the food area. We find enough chairs to be placed to support the coffin.

Chickens are bought from the neighbors for the ritual food, which must be prepared for tomorrow and for the following seven days for the *Rosarios* which will be held every afternoon. Santiago has to contract the *resadoras*, the specific village women who know how the rituals of the *Rosario* should be done. They know the songs that must be sung or chanted, petitioning the gods to allow this soul into heaven. These women must be sought, and contracted, to come each afternoon for the next eight days.

At last we have everything ready, just as the inn guests begin returning from all their adventures of the day, happy and chatting, totally unaware of what is and will happen down on the lower property edge. The body actually arrives just after the last guest is in, and it is whisked inside the palapa house. Since the one door we leave open on the hut faces away from the inn, it isn't too obvious now, but in the evening with people coming and going all night long, I wonder who will notice.

The body must never be left alone until it is buried, so the vigil begins at once. I can only be there for an hour or so, as I must attend to our guests, but Santiago will be there all night and will still have to help serve breakfast for our guests in the morning.

Somehow we pull this all off and only as they are taking the body away the next day, with half the village crowded into our narrow lane to accompany it through the streets to the cemetery, does it coincide with the departure of one set of guests. They remark on it, but do not realize it is connected to us until later.

By noon it is over and by evening all the relatives are headed out and back to their homes around the Peninsula.

*   *   *

Carmen has only one brother remaining now, Tio Pancho. He and Carmen are both even more precious to us, as we realize their time is limited too. I am not anxious for our Inn to become a funeral parlor again anytime soon.

Chapter Twenty-six
Je'ets Lu'um:
Healing the Land

Have you ever heard of a ceremony called Je'ets Lu'um?
Neither had I. This past year I was privileged to be able to see
and participate in one. The following story tells how it came
about.

*   *   *

There is a large ranch in our area that has been for sale
a couple of times over the past several years and recently
came on the market again. I use the word "ranch" loosely
because other than a deep well, a large cracked cattle
watering trough, and the remains of an old building, there
isn't much that is substantial on the acreage. The
perimeters are roughly enclosed by old rock walls and
strands of loose barbed wire, cut through in many places
where the old trails go through. The native Maya of the
village go back and forth across the land to beehives and
their fields. One trail is the old road from here to Merida,
running straight up through the middle of the peninsula.
This must be left open. People still use it, although not to
go all the way to Merida. Imagine someone just fencing off
a state highway where you live! No one would stand for it,
and they would cut the wire. It is the same here. One of the
past owners fenced it all in, creating a lot of ill will amongst
the villagers who promptly cut the fencing.

Nothing good has ever happened on the land. Project after project has failed, although they shouldn't have, until it was finally sold for losses and abandoned. It has always attracted me, this wonderful piece of land, but I am not meant to be the owner.

It is being bought by someone else now, an American couple who arrived by sheer fluke, on their first vacation to Yucatan, with no real destination in mind. The gods and the spirits in the village of Uman, to the north of us, conspired and sent them south to us, arriving on the doorstep of our small inn. In a few short days, they had made up their minds to buy this property.

Because we showed them the land, and because of the language problems, Santiago and I become the agents to put this deal together. In due time, the couple returns to explore what they have bought. Part of the land has been cleared around the main structures, and two of the men working it know the land well. Santiago is working with the men.

They advise him to do a *Primicia* or *Je'ets Lu'um*. This is a Mayan ceremony performed by a *jmeen* (pronounced, "he-men," with the accent on the "men"), meaning shaman, to "soothe the earth spirits." *Je'ets* means "to calm down" and *Lu'um* means "earth" Therefore, *Je'ets Lu'um* means, "to calm down the land." This advice is noted but not acted upon just then.

Soon after the recommendation, the new owners come out to walk the land. A short way in, the woman suddenly falls on the ground, landing hard. There is a rectangular rock next to where she had been standing. At first I think she has stumbled on the rock, but she hasn't. She was just suddenly tossed to the ground as though a giant hand had thrown her there. She isn't badly hurt, but, needless to say, she is startled. Her husband asks if she wants to continue and she decides that she would, although with a degree of obvious hesitation.

The rest of the walk is uneventful, as far as any other strange events, and presents many lovely and odd alignments. For example, two large stone entry pillars are located back behind the building ruins, leading straight into a long tree-tunnel. Looking back from mid-tunnel, you align with the entry pillars, the door in the structure, and the entry pillars by the road, a rather strange alignment. Or is it? The land has a sort of magical, spiritual quality, which you feel, an energy that runs through it.

Next, the woman's foot swells and turns dark, as though kicked by a boot. The suggestion of *Je'ets Lu'um* arises again.

There are three other ceremonies that the *jmeen* can perform on the land. One is the *ka'ax lu'um, amarar la tierra*, to tie down the earth. The *jmeen* buries objects on the four corners of the land, objects that can cause harm to an intruder on the land. The intruder may be bitten by a snake or a scorpion, or fall, or break something.

Another ceremony is the *cha chak*, where the entire village participates. Small boys are symbolically tied to the altar table's four legs and make sounds like frogs ... frogs always signifying the coming of the rainy season. The altar table preparation is attended by men only. They prepare the food for the formal *hua I col* ceremony. The *hua I col* includes the villagers who offer the proper food and drink to the gods in thanks for past harvests and to beseech them to give bountiful harvests and rain in the future.

The ceremony proposed for this particular land is *Je'ets Lu'um*, followed by a less formal *hua I col* where women can attend and participate, in order to appease and soothe the various gods and spirits that have been neglected for so long. In the *Je'ets Lu'um*, the new owners will be formally introduced by name to all the past dwellers on the land, to the many gods protecting it, and to the *Alux*—the tiny naked people the Maya believe live in the forests.

The *Alux* are not the same as the land spirits, although they are connected. The *Alux* were supposedly created by man, by a *jmeen*. They were made out of clay in the form of a small nude child and given life with the blood of the *jmeen*. They were to guard the *jmeen's* personal *milpa*, his corn field, so no one could steal his corn or crops. He later taught others how to create these *Alux*, to guard their own *milpa*. Each *jmeen* had to maintain their *Alux*, which called for a special preparation of the corn called *sak-ha*. The *Sak-ha* offering is made of corn boiled with just water, no lime (powdered limestone) until it is tender—corn to make tortillas is mixed with lime. Then it is cooled and ground fine like the drink they call *pozoli*, and then mixed with honey.

When the land the *jmeen* were going to work had been defined by cutting a wide line called a *brecha* around it, but before they had actually started working the land, the *jmeen* talked to these *Alux* to guard their land from the theft of crops or damage from nature. They also told the *Alux* to safeguard the *jmeen* from danger from, for example, snake bites or being cut by accident while using the machete, etc. The *jmeen* made, and continue to make, small personal offerings to the *Alux* to safeguard their land, crops, and themselves.

This offering is placed in four small dried gourds cut in half and positioned at the four cardinal points of the earth. It is then offered to the earth spirits—wind, rain, and sun— from each of the four cardinal points. One asks the wind to bring the rain and then the sun to make the crops grow. Each spirit is called *yum. Yum-chac* is rain, *yum-ik'* is wind, and *yum-k'in* is sun. The Mayan *yum* means *padre* in Spanish and "father" in English. It could just as well be *Yum* Indal, *Yum* Santiago. It simply means father, not as in God the Father, but father wind, father rain, father sun.

The *jmeen* created the *Alux* to guard the land, and through the offering, he asks the spirits to help him with favorable crops, so the *Alux* and earth spirits are now working together. When making the offering, the conductor of the ceremony talks to both. He explains what he is doing, and why, and *who* is doing it, so that the *Alux* will know who it is and will understand what he is doing. He can also seek help from the earth spirits, if appropriate.

Over the years, it evolved that all who made their *milpa* could talk to the *Alux* and the earth spirits, the responsibility being that farmers had to support the *Alux* with the proper offerings. The *Alux* were released when the crop was in and the harvest done. They could then be free from their responsibility to the crop and go to help others.

However, if the land is abandoned, so are the *Alux*. If they have not been properly released, nor appeased, nor given another task, they are adrift. And that is when trouble can start.

Man created these *Alux*, and therefore has the responsibility to care for them and maintain them, basically forever, or release them to someone else who is going to work the land. When someone new is going to be on the land, or work it, it is important to introduce that person to the *Alux* who are there. Even if the land has been abandoned for long periods, the *Alux* are still there, still hanging around and quite possibly rather disgruntled at being ignored. If they are not properly appeased, they begin to make their presence known to you. They want attention, they want a job, and they want you to support them properly again.

All of the ceremonies will be used to assure the *Alux* that the new owners will be respectful of the land and its formations, whether natural or created. In each ceremony, these entities will be asked to help, welcome, and protect the new owners and to ward off any malignant spirits that still linger.

To do these ceremonies, an area must be prepared for the altar and its offerings, the pits dug for baking the ceremonial bread, *piib*, and the proper food stuffs bought or found. Turkeys, chickens, *licor de cana*, cinnamon, anise spice, ground pumpkin seeds, chives, mint, pepper, honey, ground corn—all must be provided. If it is to be a proper ceremony, all these things must be done, and correctly.

It occurs to me that I am in a unique position. I am the only foreigner I know, married to a Maya, living in a still fairly traditional village here on the Peninsula, surrounded by, and able to participate in, authentic Mayan events— spiritual, cultural, family, and village events. I am not set aside, I am not gawked at. I am a part of a family who belongs here and so I have been given the chance to see, and be involved in many things the average visitor to our area would never dream existed.

I am always surprised when tourists ask me, "And what happened to all the Maya?" as they are standing among them, the Maya.

My husband, my nieces, my mother-in-law, and another of Santiago's brothers, Makim, are helping with the ceremony. Auseri, Dimetrio, Luis, Eliseo—the workers—are here. They are the Maya. They are all still here and arranging this ceremony. Not because they will earn any money from it, nor for tourism promotion, but because it needs to be done.

"Come and participate, but accept and believe. Do not scoff at us, for our beliefs are real. We are still here, we Alux, *guarding the land."*

But for now, we need to find a turkey. It is looking like we will be driving all the way to Xkol Ok, a tiny village way back behind Uxmal, to buy a turkey. It is the wrong time of the year for turkeys and no one in our village has one ready to sell. Word has it that the villagers in Xkol Ok have some. And lucky for us they do.

An enormous amount of work goes into this ceremony. Village people volunteer to help with every aspect. They dig the pits to bake the bread called *piib*, they haul water, and bring buckets, tables, and chairs. They begin making the *piib* itself.

Piib resembles a very large fat tortilla. Each one is patted out by hand from fresh ground corn. The corn has to be arranged for, ground, and hauled to this ranch, which is about two kilometers from the village center, and usually reached by bicycle or walking.

We borrow a truck on the way to the ranch and pick up people, as well as load the necessary items. While some of the men are using a couple of old shovels we have to dig the pit, which measures about three meters long, 1.5 meters wide and about 60 centimeters deep, others are gathering rock, wood, and oak leaf branches.

The women make the piib.
Photo courtesy Santiago Dominguez

When the pit is ready, it is filled with wood. The wood is lit and the rocks placed in a layer over the wood. When the fire dies down, the heated rocks fall, and they have to be moved around with long wooden poles to assure an even bed for cooking. It is a hot and arduous job. The men are drenched with sweat when they finish.

We have already made what seems like hundreds of fat tortilla *piibs*, but still there are buckets of dough yet to be formed. The American woman is helping as is a Canadian lady whom we invited to see the ceremony. Neither speak Spanish, let alone Mayan, but everyone is laughing and joking anyway. The universal language of hand signals serves to break the barriers. The foreigners' tortillas are poorly made but they are trying very diligently to help. I am pressed into service for a while and the village ladies are impressed by my *piib*. They nod and say "*suegra*" with approval, meaning my Mayan mother-in-law has taught me well. I realize I am happy for her. She will hear of it, and it will make her happy. Shortly I am called away to run more errands.

The wood in the pit is lit in preparation of making the piib. Photo courtesy Santiago Dominguez

The uncooked *piibs* are stacked, 12 to a pile, with ground pumpkin seeds between each, rather like a stack of hot cakes, and then wrapped in banana leaves. These bundles are secured with string made from henequen, a fiber produced from the agave plant. A separate group of men have been busy putting together the bundles all morning. One stack is made with 13 *piibs*. This one is to be placed by the *jmeen* himself in the cooking pit, on top of the hot leveled rocks. After this, the other men can help place the remaining bundles in the pit. When these are all arranged to their satisfaction on the hot rocks, everything is first covered with soil and then with the oak leaf branches. The men check carefully that no steam is escaping which could spoil the cooking process.

The uncooked piib are placed in banana leaves.
Photo courtesy Santiago Dominguez

After the pit gets covered over with no steam escaping, it takes about an hour and a half until it is judged "done" and the *piibs* are ready to be taken out. By then it will be afternoon.

Meanwhile the women have split into groups, some preparing the chickens and turkeys, and some the spices and condiments for cooking. Earlier, the men butchered and defeathered the birds, saving the blood for the broth to be used later. The women now prepare it all for the cooking kettle. This is an enormous pot, which we borrow especially for the ceremony. It looks like one a cannibal might use.

I have been sent to find more cilantro, chives, and mint—the cooks deciding we didn't have enough. By now I have been through half the gardens in town and gained four more volunteers to help with the work.

Carmen, left, and her daughter Pilar defeather chickens and a turkey. Photo courtesy Sheila Clark

While the *piibs* were being formed, the cooking fire was being built. The poultry and spices are now ready to be put in the broth. Everything from the poultry will go in except the entrails, lungs, and claws. Head, neck, heart, liver, etc. all go in the broth. The spices and condiments are placed in a clean cloth, tied, and submerged in the broth to flavor it, later to be removed.

Of course, another group has prepared food for us mere mortals to eat—*Frijol con puerco*, beans with pork, naturally. This is to keep us all going until the special food is ready and has been offered to the gods. Then we can partake.

The men have been out here preparing for the ceremony since 5:30 a.m., working to have the *piibs* ready to be removed from the pit by about 3:00 p.m.

The uncooked piib, wrapped in banana leaves, are stacked in piles. Photo courtesy Sheila Clark

We are almost into the rainy season, which usually brings late afternoon rain, but it hasn't begun yet. It will be wonderful if our ceremony brings the first rains ... but not before the *piib* is removed from the pit. That would be considered rather ill fortune indeed.

All has been going well. Smaller *piibs* called *Hu'o*, or *sapos* (frogs), or *niños* (children), have also been prepared. They are ready and placed in the pit. These are wrapped in

Ba'tun leaves, a plant found only in certain places, and are a special offering to the rain gods.

The *jmeen* has done the first two of three orations. The first is to start the ceremony, blessing the turkeys and chickens and the *sacah,* which is a drink of ground corn and water with bee's honey, *miel de abejas.* The second blessing occurs when the birds are cooked and placed on the offering altar. The last oration will be the *Cho K'o,* performed after all the *piib* is cooked.

Food for us mere mortals—beans with pork, of course—along with piibs, the mound to the left and back behind. Food for the mortals is in the pots: the black one and the one in the front. The buckets hold offerings for the gods.
Photo courtesy Santiago Dominguez

Looking around, I realize what a lot of goodwill and happiness there is, on everyone's part. Everyone is working together, helping to make this special ceremony for people they barely have met—the new owners of the ranch.

And at that point, I know it is all going to work, the ceremony will be a success, the gods will approve.

*　　*　　*

So did it rain? Yes. In fact, it poured. But not until the piib *was out of the pit and the last blessing was almost completed.*

On the grounds is the shell of an old building that still has a roof. It housed the chapel. When it began to sprinkle, we all gathered in there, waiting for the jmeen *and his assistants to finish the last blessing, a blessing during which women are not allowed. As he finished, it began to rain hard, so we all stayed in the shelter. One of the village men, a self-styled comedian, began to sing a Mayan love song to the Canadian woman, who had a marvelous sense of humor. Then the man began to play an invisible guitar and to sing. The new American owner happens to be a school band director. He stepped over to tune-up the invisible guitar! This made everyone roar with laughter. Looking at all the different happy faces, I knew I had rarely had a better day down here. I think the* Je'ets Lu'um *will be a success, the land calmed down, and accepting again.*

Indeed, a very special day.

Chapter Twenty-seven
A Word about Weddings

I have been to dozens of weddings since I arrived here. The first few years, hardly a week went by that an invitation didn't arrive.

*   *   *

"Invitations" can be anything from a formal card announcement to a handwritten note decorated with hand-drawn flowers. But one thing is standard. The invitation is personally presented. This includes the couple about to get married and one set of parents, sometimes a grandmother and small nieces and nephews, all going on an outing throughout the village, hand delivering each invitation. This takes several hours at the very least, as a certain amount of chit-chat is essential in each house. To cut this short would be unthinkable.

The length of the stay depends on how important you are to the family and whether or not you have been asked to be a *padrino* or *madrina* ... think of them as the good fairies of weddings. Wedding costs here are seldom, if ever, borne solely by the couple marrying or their family. Help is always sought. There are *padrinos* for the cake, the rings, the music band, the bride's dress, the beer, the souvenirs, etc. This can involve a relatively minor expense or a major one. It is somewhat difficult to refuse to be a *padrino*, and, for the major expenses, the gesture is usually offered by someone close to the family.

The family's responsibility is for the locale—the place the wedding party will be held—and involves all the food preparation and cost. Many family members help out here. The family's responsibility also includes the set-up and finding of enough tables and chairs to seat the guests, plus the actual serving and clean-up afterwards. Catering doesn't exist here—nor anyone to help with the planning. As a result, weddings can be chaotic, barely avoiding disaster, or fairly well organized, depending on the abilities of the families involved.

In recent years, Superior beer has helped out greatly. Now, if you contract with them to supply the beer, they supply the plastic chairs and tables for the event. This wasn't always so. Before, people went around in a truck or *triciclo* rounding up chairs and tables at the last minute from everyone they knew. The front half of a *triciclo* is a metal-framed, open-fronted cart with a removable wooden seat and two side wheels. Welded to the back of the cart is the back half of a bicycle. A person sits on the bicycle seat and uses the bicycle pedals to propel the *triciclo* forward. *Triciclos* move everything from livestock to people to household goods. They are an essential part of the Yucatecan rural scene.

The wedding parties are always held at the family's house, usually the bridegroom's. It is typical that the band sets up in the afternoon and blows out all the electrical circuits, all one or two of them, and someone will have to figure out a way to get the power on again. These functions never start on time, nor should you expect them to. I don't think there *is* a specific starting time. You know that the church ceremony will be on a Saturday at 5:00 p.m.

because that is when the shared priest comes to our village. It can't be any other time or day. The church ceremony itself is not valid for the legal part of the wedding, which is just a short civil service ceremony. The church "wedding" and the following reception party can take place shortly following the civil service or weeks to months later, as dictated by "urgency" and finances.

A wedding couple at the church, Yulisley on the left, Nidia (then Mimi) on the right.

At dawn on the day of the wedding party, the hosting family starts to butcher the pigs, chickens, and turkeys needed for the food dishes, which are offered in the early afternoon, as well as at night. It is quite typical that the groom's female relatives—mother, grandmother, sisters, aunts, and previous *madrinas* (such as a birth godmother)—never even get out of the cooking hut during the entire day, let alone make it to the church ceremony or

221

have time to change clothes for the party. The "formal" part is the responsibility of the bride's family and of the various wedding *madrinas*. They must show up all dressed up.

Female family members may not get out of the cooking hut.

The same goes for the *padrinos*. The men in the groom's family are running around trying to get everything all set up and doing "men things," like drinking beer and chatting. So the *padrinos* are supposed to be neatly dressed and stay sober, at least for a reasonable length of time.

Traditionally, these ceremonies are always held in the yard around the family *palapa* or small concrete house. There is never enough room but it all works out and is generally a fun-filled hilarious event of food, jokes, dancing, and good cheer. It never lasts much after midnight. There aren't any cars, so the procession to and from the church is literally through the streets, no matter what the weather. This is why most of the weddings fall between December and May, the dry season here, if at all possible. I have seen a sudden rain storm turn the wedding party into a sea of mud, soaking the beautiful gowns up to the knees with red sloppy mud, ruining everyone's shoes and clothes. And the party goes on anyway.

At a traditional wedding here in the village, it is expected that you bring a gift. You look for these gifts in the pharmacy/grocery stores, not exactly where you would expect to find them if you were from the U.S. The most acceptable items seem to be a drinking glass and shallow glass bowl combination that come in sets of two. Not four or six. Another acceptable gift would be an assortment of small metal pots and pans. Not toasters, wine glasses, fine china, crystal, or sterling silver. No linens or furniture. Remember you are talking about life in a *palapa* hut or a small concrete house where actual furniture is rare. Hammocks serve for everything—sleeping, sitting, and watching the now must–have television.

Yolanda and Cousin Doroteo's procession from the church to the house—a long way.

As mentioned before, there is usually a small plywood wardrobe with front doors made of mirrors. One side is used for hanging (and piling up) clothes and the other side has drawers. This is pretty much standard. There is one table which serves as an altar/shrine and TV/stereo holder. And that's it for the sleeping/living quarters.

The cooking area is generally detached and, quite commonly, a separate *palapa* hut, even if the actual house is of concrete blocks. The cooking hut is the heart of the household activity until after the main meal is over. It is for this area that you are purchasing a gift.

Cousin Doroteo's wedding reception in the yard with the band.

It took me a while to understand this, so our first gifts were pretty much useless—a set of four lovely hand-blown drinking glasses and a beautiful painted ceramic bowl ... perfectly useless and probably put away for safe keeping or broken within the first week by some small hand. Instead, a set of plastic Tupperware bowls would have been greatly appreciated. Yes, I made a few errors, but I have learned. Now I let Santiago do the buying!

You also never ever wrap these in fancy paper. The little store puts your gift on a gift-paper-covered piece of cardboard, places clear plastic wrap over the top, and shrink wraps it with a hairdryer. This is so everyone can see what the loot is, all piled on a table by the cake for all to admire, never mind that three-fourths of the gifts are all the same!

Furthermore, there are no cards indicating who gave what nor will you ever get a thank you, verbal or otherwise. It simply isn't done, much to the astonishment and dismay of some foreigners.

Cousin Doroteo and his bride Yolanda in his thatch hut.

There is a story about a man who was the manager of one of the nearby large tourist hotels. When one of his more important staff members got married, this manager gave them a new double bed with linens included and had it delivered to the village. He was extremely miffed when the couple never even thanked him. In truth, a double bed would almost touch all sides of the *palapa* hut the couple had built to live in, separate from the groom's parents house, and there was no way they could have used the bed or wanted to. They sleep in hammocks. Everyone does. The manager retired a couple of months later, and the couple sold the bed and bought the wardrobe they needed. I know it's true because I was at the wedding.

The food served at the wedding party is also standardized. It is always tacos, about five for each person, made from shredded pork and turkey meat. There is also a cooked potato and carrot salad with mayonnaise.

Beverages are Coke, Orange Crush, and beer. The cake, no matter how big, is *tres leches*, three milks, with a meringue frosting. The meringue colors are white with powder blue accents. I have never seen anything different.

Guests waiting for food at Cousin Doroteo's wedding.

The more elaborate weddings used to be held in the *cancha*, the inner courtyard behind the *palacio*, the local government building with all the arches. This courtyard serves for school graduations, meetings, basketball games, and other activities. In the past, it could be used for weddings, provided you had a personal connection with the village president. However, some years ago one wedding got out of control so permission was revoked, never to be granted again.

For a while, a large empty area behind one of the local houses was rentable. But alongside it was the local cantina. The drunks mixing with the wedding party proved to be unpopular, and it fell into disuse. As the home property became subdivided, small pieces going to each marrying son, the home grounds eventually became too small to host most weddings. An alternative location was sought.

The choice was the *comisaría*. This is a metal-roofed, covered, concrete structure originally built as a packing plant for okra, a vegetable meant to be raised and shipped to the U.S. This project was never really successful.

The bridesmaids serving food and beverages at Cousin Doroteo's wedding.

The *comisaría* has a couple of concrete buildings. It served as the preparatory school for three years until the new school was built. It is mainly used today for occasional *ejido campesino* (farmers meetings), for weddings, and *Quince Años* celebrations.

*   *   *

Now, weddings are not what they used to be. About the time they started using the comisaría *structure, the taste in music changed as "rap crap" began to filter down from the U.S. After the traditional music and bride's waltz, or the* quinceañeras *waltz, at about midnight, the music would change, becoming loud heavy-metal, throbbing-drum "noise," lasting until around 3:00 a.m., with speakers way too big. This lasted a number of years and then began to wane causing the adults of the village to rejoice. Some couples still choose it, but many are going back to the more traditional music—music you can actually dance to, instead of just jump up and down.*

I didn't realize I had been avoiding weddings and Quince Años *for quite some time. The celebrations at the* comisaría *had no personality, no warmth—not to mention the noise level—and so I began inventing excuses not to attend.*

The author at yet another wedding.

Our first family wedding in many years here in the village came as a surprise. Nephew Wilbur got married in a civil service ceremony and, opting to forego the Saturday church wedding, had scheduled Friday as the wedding party day, largely because both he and his father had gotten the day off from their construction jobs in Merida. It was a lovely cool evening, and I had almost forgotten how much fun an old fashioned family function, held in the yard, could be. Tables were set up anywhere and everywhere. Little kids ran around crazy, inventing their own games. Everyone in the family helped in one way or another. Sure enough, the small band blew out the circuits, and Santiago had to patch in a line from the neighbor's to get the band and lights working again.

There was no real "time" to show up. People got there at 5:00 p.m. and people arrived at 10:00 p.m. A pretty good time to arrive is 7:00 p.m. Sure enough, there were all the plastic-wrapped gifts piled up on the table, next to the white with blue meringue covered cake. Out came the five shredded pork and turkey tacos followed by the cooked carrot, potato, and mayonnaise salad. Beer and Coke and Orange Crush. Ah yes, I had forgotten. What fun.

Santiago and I started everybody dancing at about 9:00 p.m. Someone always has to get things rolling, and it usually falls to us if we are attending. After about a half hour ... and more beer ... things began to roll along by themselves. Soon everyone was dancing. Funny thing was, it never seemed to get out of hand. You expended tons of energy serving, dancing, and helping, and nobody ever seemed to get drunk. By midnight everyone started leaving, as if at some invisible signal. Grandmothers and little kids were packed off to bed, extra food was parceled out to departing guests, and it was all over. Everyone had fun. New lives were starting.

I miss the old style weddings.

Chapter Twenty-eight
The Fabric of Life

The fabric of life is changing here. When I first arrived, and for many, many years prior to that, everything centered on the family and the milpa—*the small farming plots each family has. Very early every morning, the men and boys of the family left for the* milpa. *There are no horses here, so the main mode of transportation was bicycles and walking, rifle slung over the shoulder. You might get lucky and shoot some game that day—a* Chachalaka *(a large game bird similar to a Grouse), a wild pig, or maybe even a deer if your land was far enough out in the hills,* el monte.

Things have changed a lot since then.

$$* \qquad * \qquad *$$

There are only a couple areas around certain fields that have a communal well that the government has dug, where water can be drawn out to irrigate the crops. The depth of the water table varies greatly on the Peninsula. Drilling in our area is very expensive and laborious, and not always successful, so there are few wells here. Where there is a communal well, you have a turn, a day, a certain number of hours a week, of water usage. The electricity is very expensive so even if the farmers have the right to this water, they may not use it because they can't pay the cost.

Around our village, you have a turn for water usage. The irrigation channels are hard-packed dirt furrows between the crops. The crops are primarily corn, various beans, and peanuts. At times watermelon and tomatoes are grown also. A great deal of this is just for home consumption, and little is left over to sell. Families' needs come first.

Many farmers supplement their income by beekeeping. This region produces several kinds of honey. Much of it is exported if it is high enough quality. My favorite is from the flower of the plant they call *Ts'iits'ilche*, the honey of which is light in color and has a delicate, slightly orange flavor. Every year, someone brings me a liter bottle of it, which I treasure. The tahonal daisy-like flower and the *jabin* tree, with its small sweet flower clusters, are also important sources of honey for this region. When the *jabin* trees are in bloom, you hear the sound of bees buzzing everywhere.

The village has a couple of tractors for tilling and preparing the land. The tractors are used after last year's crop residue has been burned. The ash is a source of nutrients for future crops. Burning also rids the fields of bugs and insects.

The farming areas are widely spread out in the valleys between the hills and not visible from the highway around our village. They are anywhere from two to seven kilometers from the town—quite a hike in this climate. Each farming area is composed of a group of men called *socios* who have their plots of land in that area. Each group is a small society of men and can be quite powerful within the village political structure.

Women do not have fields in this area, but they are the ones, with their younger sons, whose job it is to go into the hills and cut *leña*, the cooking firewood, from dead trees.

You can see them in the late afternoon, returning with tumplines (cloth straps) around their heads, shouldering large bundles of cut sticks for their cooking fires. They appear out of the scrub jungle from invisible trails, like apparitions, stepping suddenly out onto the road. This job also falls to the elderly men. It continually amazes me how strong they all are, to support such bundles, walking long distances back to the town in this heat.

Planting is done in the age-old way, by poking a sharpened stick into the ground, dropping in a seed, tamping the dirt over with your foot, and continuing. Machines don't sow seed. Neither do they weed, water, or harvest here. People do. When a big crop is ready, everybody in the family goes out to help.

There is laughter and joking. The soft lilting Mayan language floats and soars in the air. The Mayan language is lovely to listen to. It always reminds me of music, music with almost an African flare to it with a wonderful cadence. I have been surrounded by it for the last nineteen years, as it, not Spanish, is the language of the interior of the Peninsula, and yet I have learned little more than words and phrases. It is not an easy language to learn.

Whereas the men rule in the fields, the women rule in the cooking *palapas.* Cooking is still done over open fires. Meat is broiled on skewers of green wood off to the side. The grill is used to cook the tortillas, which are made from fresh ground corn, after the meal is cooked.

Food stuffs that the family doesn't have are purchased fresh every morning at the local market. Only what can be eaten that day is cooked. Meals can be quite meager if a family is very poor, but there are always tortillas and chilies. There is one main meal a day, eaten around 1:00 or 2:00 p.m. In the later afternoon, it is bath time for everyone.

The cooking *palapa* is the heart of the family, at least until after the meal. Here the women and girls spend most of their hours preparing and cooking the meal, gossiping and discussing village events. They are also *desgranando* the corn ears, removing the dried corn kernels from the husks by rubbing them together, a job not as easy as it looks, and which can take hours. These kernels are then boiled in a powdered lime and water mixture to soften them and remove the coarse outer shell before grinding the next day.

While one girl hand washes the family clothes in the *batella*, an aggregate wash sink, and hangs them to dry, another is sent to the *molino* to get the corn ground, and yet another to buy whatever the family needs for that day's meal.

In our village, everyone has their own chickens to slaughter, but most buy the pork they need daily from whomever has slaughtered a pig in the wee hours of the morning. Your own pigs and turkeys are saved for special occasions or raised to sell for other things that are needed. Only a few people raise cattle, and only one is slaughtered per week. As a result, beef is only available on Saturday in the early morning.

Children are not really pushed to stay in school, especially the girls, as they are needed to help out in the family. The little boys go to the fields to help their father or uncles. Many of the girls are not allowed to go further than sixth grade as they will be of marriageable age soon. It is quite typical of women here to have no more than one or two years of school.

When a girl marries, she goes to the new husband's family and becomes part of the fabric of that family. And of course, when a son marries, that family inherits a new daughter. It is very rare that the new couple would move out of, or away from, the village. This extended family means that there is never a shortage of help and comfort. There is always someone to care for the children and the old or infirm, plus people to share the burdens of work. It works very well. It is a very secure feeling.

Now this way of life is being threatened. In the past, we had several village men who worked construction, on highways or buildings, in Merida or around Cancun. They would return every two weeks, or once a month, for a day, perhaps two, and go back on the bus to work. If the need arose, another brother, cousin, or uncle was always around to help the women of the family. Whether it was cutting down a tree, rebuilding the rock property walls called *albarradas*, or fixing the one light in the sleeping *palapa*, some family member was there, available to help.

A few years ago, the migration to the north began—men going over the border, seeking work. Most often this was to California. The men from each village would get established in a certain area and would slowly build their own community within a community. Speaking their own language, preparing their own food dishes, they left behind wives and mothers, sisters, aunts, and children.

So the women were left alone, and the children began to grow up with no fathers, no uncles, and no older brothers. Women moved back to their mothers' houses to share responsibilities and chores and child care, and to not be alone.

The men sent back money, a great deal in comparison to what they had before, and new businesses arose because of it. Construction material businesses boomed, as everyone started building a new concrete block house. Avon products became a big seller, as women now had money to buy frivolities. Clothing styles changed and the traditional white embroidered dress, the *huipil*, was replaced by modern dresses, and jeans and tee shirts for the young. Modest plastic sandals gave way to high platform shoes. Nail polish became the rage along with permanent hair waves and hair coloring.

Everyone had to have a washing machine now, even if it could only wash one pair of jeans at a time. A refrigerator was a must (with nothing but Coke inside, usually to sell). You might even want to buy a stove—the oven being a good place to store your new dishes.

Furniture could be bought "on time," in payments, as well as pots and pans, and salesmen appeared as if by magic. Never mind what the people needed or could use, or were ready for, these items were bought. Huge stereo/radio sets and TV's were the first major purchases on the list. Where to put them in the *palapa* sleeping hut did not matter. Space would be found. The altar/saints table had to do double duty ... and did.

No one wanted to work in the *milpa* anymore. It was much easier and more profitable to go over the border and wash dishes. The times, they were a' changing.

Those who came back with money opened new clothing stores and construction supply stores to meet the demand.

Stores expanded their wares. People began selling chickens because it was easier to buy one plucked and ready than to chase, kill, and pluck your own for the noon meal.

Bands of young boys, growing up with no fathers' discipline, were out on the prowl. Delinquency reared its ugly head, but not for long. Calls went out, and when fathers or older brothers came home, the troublemakers were on the next trip north to earn money. And so crime sort of passed us by.

Yuli's sixth grade graduation.

This flow to the north killed much of the inspiration for the boys to stay in school—why dilly-dally away preparing for jobs that would only pay 50 to maybe 100 pesos per day when you could be washing dishes in San Francisco tomorrow, earning more in one hour than in a whole day here!

For some of the girls, the migration has provided an unforeseen opportunity—the chance to continue their education. If there are no boys to marry, and fewer family babies to care for, then you might as well stay in school. So our girls have been given a chance too. Several have now completed preparatory school and gone on to a tech college, computer school, teaching school, or nursing school. But we also lose them this way, as this takes them out of the village. Most never return except to visit.

The girls were some of the first in the village to graduate from secondary school and go on to graduate from preparatory. Here Nidia, right, receives awards at her secondary graduation.

After five years of a steady northern flow, the fabric of the village has changed. The U.S. dollar now speaks loudly but still doesn't shriek. Kids have brand new bicycles and clothes, unheard of before. The division is growing between the haves and the have-nots—those with U.S. money and those without. Many small children have never seen their fathers and know only a voice over the telephone or a face on a videotape. Women are reforming and arranging their own lives as their men stay away longer and are not always happy to be back again under the thumb of their husband when he does return. For some women though, this has given them new opportunities to learn and grow, taking on responsibilities that formerly only the men would do. So far, the pattern has been that the men stay no longer than four to six months in the village after returning from the U.S. When they run out of money, they head north again. Few have yet to come back and stay, but those who have returned and stayed have done very well in their new businesses.

*   *   *

There is a tiny farming community way back in the Puuc hills about an hour from here that we found on a Sunday drive. What was startling was that almost every thatch palapa *house had a new, large, elaborate concrete house being built right beside it, each with the most amazing, huge, carved, double black-wood entry door! Truly elegant, almost all the same design, in a village that time almost forgot. It is only because of the U.S. dollars rolling in that enables these people to buy these outstanding wooden doors for their new houses. What will happen to this village in the future? Who will continue to tend the fields?*

And what will happen to ours?

Chapter Twenty-nine
Una Vela Mas:
Doña Carmen

Doña Carmen.

We will have a new candle on the altar for the days of the dead this year. Carmen, Santiago's mother and the girls' grandmother, will die within the next 24 hours or sooner. She went downhill very suddenly and asked to be brought back to her own little thatch hut to "leave from my own house." So last night we brought her back from Antonio's house where she has been, safe from the hurricanes and storms. We had been using her little house to store goods for the new rooms we are building for the inn, so she is in among boxes of tile, water heaters, electrical wire, and plumbing supplies. Her special saint, once again, is back in its place. She sees none of it. Her spirit seems to have already gone. We are just waiting for her body to follow.

The girls and Santiago have all come to me, one by one, seeking comfort, each trying to be strong for the other, trying not to show their tears. But none of us can control that—Carmen has meant too much to all of us.

Remembering Carmen and her beautiful embroidery.

We have her best dress laid out, one she made, and her *fustán*, underskirt, and the meter of white cloth that she will be wrapped in. I have the 11 white candles and will soon go to buy Nescafe coffee, sugar, and the cookies for the all-night vigil that will follow her death. The cookies, called *Marias* and *Soles*, and animal crackers are deemed most appropriate, along with the soft drinks of Pepsi, Orange Crush, and *Cebada*, which is a barley drink.

Cebada is a local/regional drink that is mostly made in the home. It is not sold commercially in the supermarkets, but many times you can find it sold on the streets from venders who make it themselves. It is wildly popular down here and also used to make Popsicles.

Carmen loved the seashore.

Everything is ready. The table for the vigil, the white cloth for wrapping her body, the 11 candles in glass jars with pictures of the saints' images.

The Catholic religion and Maya beliefs are so mixed here that some of the rituals don't seem true to either religion but are a whole new tradition altogether. However, some customs seem to have greater effect than others, among those being the "last rites."

Carmen is Maya to the core. She never wears anything except the traditional hand-embroidered (by herself) *huipil* dress. Her feet are deformed by years of work so that she can wear nothing except a thong-like sandal. Her long hair

243

is always braided and pinned up. She refuses to wear glasses, saying it makes her look too old. She wears a necklace and medallion that I made for her years ago and simple, small hoop earrings. That is all the jewelry she has ever had. She refuses to be buried with anything except her dress, wrapped in a meter and a half of white percale cotton cloth.

She speaks only Mayan, but she loves certain TV soap operas that, of course, are in Spanish. She watches them every day she can. She also recites long prayers and parts of the Bible in Latin that she learned in church as a child. So her beliefs are a strange mix of Catholic and Mayan. We are ready for the last rite rituals, whenever she goes.

However, Carmen will not let go. By the second day she has slipped into a kind of coma, and her breathing is terribly harsh. Everyone in the family has arrived, and she is never alone. We close the inn, putting out a sign saying we are repainting. By evening, it becomes obvious that she is waiting for something, some trigger to let her go. Her sons and daughter, grandchildren, and friends are all with her. Santiago finally decides to bring a *resadora*, a woman who recites traditional prayers, to the house. He thinks maybe it will bring Carmen the peace she needs.

There have been three deaths in the village that same day—unusual. We find that all the proper *resadoras* are already taken. There are none left to come to us. Normally these prayers are started just after death, after the body has been cleansed and dressed and placed in the casket.

Out of sheer desperation, Santiago goes to see Cousin Leon, who worked for years as caretaker and assistant to the priest at our huge Catholic Church. Leon finally agrees to come, not liking to go out after dark because he is afraid of spirits. But for Carmen he will come. He gathers all her children and grandchildren around and recites what is actually a Catholic ritual. As he starts to speak in Spanish, her breathing becomes quiet. At the words, "The Father, The Son, and The Holy Ghost," she gives a little sigh ... and leaves. It is the sign she has been waiting for.

Her sons all go to the cemetery on the eighth day after her death. This is the day they believe the soul departs from earth and is an emotional day for all. It is a way for the earth-bound to give a final good-bye to the person that they love.

Remembering Carmen making tortillas in the cooking hut. Photo courtesy Sheila Clark

We have now had 11 days of *Rosarios*, special prayer sessions, led by certain village women; one session for each of the 11 candles that we light. These three women come every afternoon to pray for Carmen's soul and to ask for it to be admitted to heaven. One of these days is devoted to her mother and father, one to her deceased daughter and dead husband, and the last three days to all her other deceased relatives.

Everyone has now been honored. Three of these days involve special foods prepared by her daughter Pilar, her nieces, and neighbors. These days are the day after death, eight days after death when everyone gathers again, and the final 11th day.

*   *   *

There will be another Rosario *held at seven weeks when everyone who can will come again, one at six months, and one at the year anniversary of her death. Each ritual will involve specially prepared foods. Each year thereafter there will be a* Rosario *on the day of her death. Her altar will be set up with the proper foods and candles, and flowers will be taken to the cemetery.*

We will remember Carmen as she wanted.

Chapter Thirty
Water!

There is nothing like the sound of a big machine moving down the highway. You feel it before you see it, a deep throaty rumble that vibrates the earth.

And it is coming towards us.

We have just arrived from a long day in Merida, spent getting money—stacks of money, an *Iman* (a magnetic device that breaks down scales formed by hard water), and prices on submersible pumps and PVC tubing. We pass the three little boys who work for us as we drive in. They are heading towards home, but not for long. They are now running back up the hill, and so are we.

We are drilling a well!

The big truck, a well-drilling rig, is about to reach the slope of our small street, and if we have measured correctly, it will pass between our concrete property wall and the neighbor's old rock wall, the *albarrada*, with nothing to spare. We are all holding our breath, watching. It passes with not even a hair's space to be seen between truck and wall, tires touching the *albarrada*, moving as slow as a snail for the last thirty meters.

Now, can it get into the clearing we have been frantically working on for the past three days? Starting Easter Sunday, all of us—the girls, our garden man, the three neighbor boys (age eight to ten), plus three men from the village—have been cutting, clearing, and burning tree debris. We have also been removing big rocks by hand to form the space this rig needs to get in, turn, and work. It is Wednesday, and here it is.

We have never had a well. They are very rare in this area. We are in the one region of the whole Yucatan Peninsula where you have to dig deepest to hit water. We rely heavily on rain water. In Merida, the water table is 15 to 20 meters. Nearby Ticul and Muna are around 15 to 35 meters. Even Bolonchen to the south is not that deep. Bolonchen means "nine wells"—*bolon* is "nine" and *chen* is "well," in the Yucatecan Mayan language. These nine wells were made long, long ago by hand labor. This was possible because the water is not that deep.

We, however, must go between 65 and 80 meters before getting a good strong supply of water. In the past, we have seen two government rigs give up after three months of effort, because they could not break through the rock, destroying two giant bore bits in the process. Drilling is a horrendously long, noisy, and expensive proposition, easily lasting two to three months.

Just by chance, we had one section of our land water witched by a friend who was visiting last February. He found what seemed to be a vein of water. To find it, he made an elongated U from a piece of metal rebar, left over from a construction project, leaving the ends sticking out horizontally as handles. The U is supposed to go straight down where there is water, swinging back up again once past it. When he passed over a specific place on our land, even the force of his big hands could not stop this U from swinging down. You could see the indentations from the rebar left in his palms afterwards.

We are going to dig exactly there.

The gods looked our way again. Through happenstance, a Venezuelan rig working out of Cancun was in town drilling a well for a group that had purchased land outside the village. Getting lost at the edge of the village, the engineer stopped at the Chac Mol restaurant across the road. Owner Miguel gave them directions and offered to show them the way personally. Miguel, knowing of our dream of having a well, ran here to get Santiago, who went with them.

And so, after nineteen years, we are getting a well. The engineers say it will probably take three days to reach 70 to 80 meters, if it goes like the other site. And then the rig and crew are on to Tabasco.

The three-man crew starts drilling at 9:50 a.m. and work straight through until 2:43 p.m., reaching 40 meters. They are now saying it could be possible to hit deep water by 10:00 p.m. Hard to believe. The engineers have left to see about another job in the area, and the crew is taking a break to eat. The little boys (and all the big boys too!) are hanging around, available to do anything they can to get close to the action. "Gofers." The crew requests ice, water, Coke, Superglue (haven't a clue why), and wire.

The wind has favored us today and is barely blowing. The fine dust that we were warned about has not become too invasive. The crew looks like ghosts, covered with fine powdered limestone dust, but they have refused our offer of face masks. Too "sissy" I suspect. I would hate to see their lungs.

The white dust comes out of the hole as they drill. The dust is powdered limestone—the main composition of the

Peninsula. The shaft they are boring is eight inches in diameter, down which they will insert a six-inch heavy PVC casing, leaving four inches of space for the water to be pumped up through.

The girls on staff, the yardman, and the small boys have a million questions about this process and about the difference between other types of wells in the area. More astute questions than I would have thought. Some I can answer, the rest we ask the engineers and crew.

Everyone here wonders how much money they make, so we multiply out what each well is costing by how many wells they are drilling in the area. We subtract how much diesel they are using from the large containers they brought in at 6:00 a.m., and the probable cost of room and board.

We figure the engineer who is overseeing the project probably earns 5,000 pesos per week ($416 US) but he is responsible for housing and food, however minimal, for the workers during the job. The workers probably earn around 3,000 pesos per week ($250 US). By contrast, a typical *albanil*, house construction worker, would make from 900 to 1,500 pesos per week ($75 to $125 US), with only the lead man, who may be the only one who can read and write, earning more. This man will earn tops, 2,000 pesos ($167 US) per week here in the village, but could earn 3,000 to 4,000 pesos in Merida. His housing and food are deducted from that. They work five and a half days a week.

The children are learning math but they don't realize it, it is just a game. They ask who earns the most money and we tell them who (the engineers) and why (schooling). Just perhaps this will trigger one of them to stay on in school and come back someday to tell us, "I'm an engineer."

The crew begins work again at 23 minutes before 4:00 p.m. At 4:45, and 63 meters, no one wants to leave for any reason, certain we will hit water any time. The soil is now coming out moist.

At 5:38 p.m. and 66 meters, we have *water!* They have hit the deeper channel, and the crew is very pleased. They go another three meters more leaving us with a deep vein of water. Santiago has a grin that might split his face, which is now covered with dust. At 7:00 p.m., they are completely finished drilling—only nine hours!

*   *   *

As if this were not enough, the butterflies are back, arriving as if by magic this afternoon. The butter-yellow ones, the lime-green ones, and a new one—charcoal grey with turquoise-blue and white on its wings. Dozens of them. The little kids are already cutting their tree branch swatters. The butterfly game will start early this year. I wonder if the water brought them.

Chapter Thirty-one
Change, No Change

The village has reached a new peak. I have seen it go from bicycles to *triciclos* to motor scooters as the main mode of transportation. Everyone seems to have a moto now. You commonly see three to four people on each— older daughter driving, small child standing on the running board in front of her, mother behind holding yet another small child. No helmets, hardly safe at all, but it is much faster than walking.

We also have a new "Super Che" in Ticul, much to the delight of everyone. This is a chain of grocery stores, of Lebanese origin, that began in Jalapa, Veracruz, that now extends across much of Mexico, known formally by the name of Chedraui. The smaller stores are called simply "Super Che."

Weekends are always crowded, none more so than the *quincena* (fifteen days) payday. On these days, the line for the cashiers can extend back half-way through the first aisles of goods.

The line for tortillas at the back of Super Che can easily have twenty people waiting. Many people buy only tortillas. Stacks and stacks of them. They are around half the price the *molinos* charge, the places that grind corn to make dough, from which you can make your own tortillas or buy them already made. Our family uses about one-half kilo for each noon meal, a small amount compared to average local consumption. Most families use at least one kilo of tortillas per meal. Some families even eat two kilos, or almost a pound, at the main afternoon meal.

Also popular is the bakery. You can now get decorated cakes and donuts, as well as French-bread loaves, every day of the week.

On weekends, many people from outlying small villages hire the new local car taxis and all come into the market and Super Che. Whole families dressed in their best, crammed into one car, reminding me of the clown acts in circuses of old.

Often, people come just to look. There is a new exhibit of swimwear and goggles, something never seen before. What might they be? A whole row of cereal choices, some of which are chocolate! An entire aisle of cosmetics, shampoo, and deodorant. Large dolls in their own cardboard and plastic boxes. None of these things existed outside of Merida before. Dishware, glasses in colors, pots and pans—dozens of choices. Potato peelers. Radios and big screen televisions. The men and boys stand and watch the televisions while the women shop. Big shiny new motorcycles. So many things to see, all in one place, all new to many. Before, these items would have been purchased on a small scale at local stores (with little or no choice) or at fairs as they came through the villages at Saints Days festivals.

But people still go across to the local market to buy their meat and poultry products, vegetables and fruits, not trusting the pre-packaged goods. The market people were afraid that the Super Che would ruin their businesses, but it hasn't. People still prefer to buy their fresh goods from venders they know. Packaged bread may be okay, but a chicken breast is not.

And so it seems that the old saying, "The more things change, the more they stay the same," is true.

It is almost kite-flying time again as April comes to a close. The winds are getting stronger. The boys are out in the streets, staking out their kite-flying spots.

The men are burning their fields of stubble in preparation for the spring planting, hoping to hit it right between when it is too early and when it is almost too late.

Soon the school children will start practicing their dances and speeches for the school closure graduations.

Pigs are still led through the streets. Everyone still has chickens and roosters. You still see live turkeys, with their legs tied to prevent escape, for sale in the markets at all holidays. The ladies still make all the traditional sweets for the Days of the Dead, Christmas, and New Year's.

Family fiestas are still the heart of the village. These have not been replaced by movies, malls, or even television programs.

Maybe some people have new, elaborate concrete block houses with incredibly ornate wooden doors, but look closely and you will see the wooden pole/slat cooking huts out behind. Grandmother and Aunty still wear their handmade *huipils*. Most mothers still breastfeed their babies in the age-old way, everywhere and anywhere, so naturally.

Everyone stills bathes around 3:00 to 4:00 p.m. and is spiffy and clean by 5:00 p.m. Men still go to the center of town to gossip with their friends. Ladies still walk to the market in the morning and grind corn for the day's meal.

We may have more roads, but we still work the fields. We still believe in the *Alux* and make certain they are appeased. We have our shamans. We honor and remember our dead ... and more than once a year. We talk to them, we put flowers and candles out for them, we include them in our conversations. Do you?

The author wearing a traditional Oaxacan (Mexican) gown.

Children still help with all household chores, cheerfully. They want to work. They grow up independent, self-reliant, and happy. They go to market and buy, learn to pay, and count change correctly. They take care of each other, of those younger, and of the old ones.

These are the reasons our men and boys still come back to this familiar territory. Home.

I can think of no place on earth I would rather be than here. Here, where our souls are alive, and our minds and hands are busy ... busy making our future.

*   *   *

This book has no end. It can't. I am still here and events are still happening. Some of them may write themselves and ask to be recorded in the future. So perhaps other chapters will follow. That, of course, is up to the gods.

Kristine Ellingson
Somewhere in the Yucatan peninsula.

About the Author

**Kristine Ellingson and
Santiago Dominguez.**

Kristine grew up in small towns in eastern Oregon where people mainly made their living through ranching or the timber industry. As an adult, she moved to Portland where she briefly taught high school before becoming a jewelry designer and manufacturer. Several years later, she moved to Yucatan, Mexico, where she and her Mayan husband started a water purification plant. They eventually turned it into a bed and breakfast boutique hotel, the Flycatcher Inn, which they operate with two of their nieces.

Kristine invents new business opportunities for her and her family and educates her girls to see these opportunities where someone else might not. She believes in women and wants them to be strong and versatile. Her son and husband get along fine because they are strong men, and they accept women like her and her girls.

Kristine continues to live in the same village with her husband Santiago and her nieces.

If you would like to contact Kristine, please email her at info@suntopaz.com.

Also from SunTopaz, *www.SunTopaz.com*

DVD: *Yucatan Travel: Cancun to Chichen Itza.* Do you wonder what to expect when you visit Mayan ruins, Caribbean beaches, and Colonial cities? Are you curious about traveling among the peaceful Maya? Join Yucatan traveler Miriam Balsley as she explores Cancun, Coba, Tulum, Chichen Itza, Valladolid, Izamal, Ek Balam, Cozumel, Akumal, and Playa del Carmen.
ISBN: 978-0-9754691-9-4

BOOK: *Have Your Heart's Desire Tools for a Wealthier, Healthier, Happier Life.* Are you interested in a book that will change your life? Audience members at author Carol Chapman's speaking events love these prayers for personal transformation and self improvement. First in the "Your Spiritual Awakening" Series.
ISBN 978-0-9754691-3-2

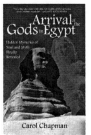

BOOK: *Arrival of the Gods in Egypt: Hidden Mysteries of Soul and Myth Finally Revealed.* While searching for clues that Atlanteans visited Egypt, an amazing series of coincidences brings the author to Asyut, a town forbidden to foreigners, where apparitions of the Virgin Mary are appearing.
ISBN: 978-0-9754691-5-6

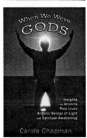

BOOK: *When We Were Gods: Insights on Atlantis, Past Lives, Angelic Beings of Light and Spiritual Awakening.* The remarkable true story of a spiritual awakening. Shocking past life regres-sion memories of Atlantis lead to a search of Mayan ruins for indications that Atlanteans visited Yucatan.
ISBN: 978-0-9754691-1-8

CPSIA information can be obtained at www.ICGtesting.com
Printed in the USA
BVOW082212040112

279759BV00005B/2/P